Effective Trusts

Minimising Disputes Through Design, Governance and Administration

Authors
Todd D Mayo and Kevin W Rethore

Managing director
Sian O'Neill

Effective Trusts: Minimising Disputes Through Design, Governance and Administration
is published by

Globe Law and Business Ltd
3 Mylor Close
Horsell
Woking
Surrey GU21 4DD
United Kingdom
Tel: +44 20 3745 4770
www.globelawandbusiness.com

Printed and bound by Severn, Gloucester, UK

Effective Trusts: Minimising Disputes Through Design, Governance and Administration

ISBN 9781787428812
EPUB ISBN 9781787428829
Adobe PDF ISBN 9781787428836

Table of contents

Acknowledgements

Todd Mayo
Like all accomplishments, writing this book was possible only thanks to the contributions of many people. I wish to highlight a few of those individuals.

I am deeply grateful to Madeleine. Since our fortuitous dinner at Houlihan's – which seems like yesterday – we've been on an incredible journey. I'm immensely better for all the time we've been together. I also am deeply grateful to Cameron, Bryn, Alistair, Phi, Lucy and Josefine, who share so much fun and laughter. And I am deeply grateful to my mom and dad, who gave me the keys that opened so many doors.

I am grateful to Sarah, Rashad, Nick and Terry, who generously shared their time and wisdom. I am fortunate to work with so many incredible people. I'm grateful to Ann Bjerke, who (among other things) made it possible for me to write this book. And Brad Dillon, who read the drafts.

And, of course, I am especially grateful to my good friend Kevin. Things are always more fun done with friends.

Prost!

Kevin Rethore

To Harry D McMunigal, Joe O'Neill and Timothy E Hoeffner – each of whom provided me with constructive guidance, support and unfiltered advice at various stages of my career. None were compelled to do so by a firm initiative or formal programme. They did so because the opportunity and will to share insights were there. Whether you did so over coffee, in the halls outside a courtroom, in an airport lobby or simply by setting an example from which to learn in critical situations, I appreciate and am indebted to each of you for your mentorship.

Special thanks to Sara Schroter, Nick Holland, Terry Franklin and Rashad Wareh – each of whom shared meaningful time with us to provide their insights and perspectives – and to my co-author Todd Mayo, who has served many significant roles over the years, perhaps none more important to me than trusted confidante and friend.

Finally, to Misiu – who faithfully ventured outside to my office to check on me, no matter what the weather. While your ulterior motives were at times quite transparent, your wagging tail and abundant energy never failed to encourage me while writing. During seemingly endless periods of pandemic-induced quarantine, the affection and loyalty of a golden retriever proved essential to our family. Thanks, pal.

I. Introduction

Trust disputes can be tremendously costly, by any number of measures. Legal fees, the cost of hiring experts and other professional service providers, as well as opportunity costs and the emotional costs associated with the highly charged atmosphere that can pit family members against one another, can add up quickly. Despite this high toll, trust litigation continues to increase – both in the number of matters being initiated and the amounts in controversy – as trust instruments become increasingly important vehicles in the management and transfer of wealth. Though the specific battlegrounds continue to evolve, a core group of issues manifest themselves from year to year.

Experience is often the best teacher, of course, and in the legal context little has the potential to educate more than trial experience. Leveraging the insights gained from instituting and defending trust litigation can provide ample and effective guidance for trustees and other fiduciaries to achieve what should be a primary goal: avoiding disputes in the first place.

Preventing a fire is substantially less costly than fighting one. Towards that end, thoughtful design and creation of a trust instrument, and well-considered processes for trust administration, can reduce the potential for trust disputes.

This book aims to provide insight into current trends and common problems fuelling trust litigation, outline potential steps to mitigate the risk of disputes, and provide guidance as to how to manage litigation when it arises.

1. Trends in trust disputes

1.1 Deep fakes and the metaverse

Though global health concerns have rightfully taken centre stage since the advent of trust litigation, trends specifically attributable to the COVID-19 pandemic have yet to emerge with clarity. This is how one trust litigator puts it:

> *[S]ome of the issues [being seen now] are the result of the fact that we live in a world of deep fakes and metaverses ... people trying new ways to create false documents ... and clever new ways for people to fraudulently take advantage of those who are controlling funds or who are trustees of trusts. Those are things we've seen on an increasing basis.*[1]

The proliferation of digital assets, technological advances and pandemic-fuelled social acclimatisation to the remote and virtual conduct of business may be contributing to this modern take on a very old theme.

> *We've [also] been seeing claims like intentional interference with expected inheritance, that have continued to grow across the country as a tort in those spaces where questions about traditional ways of attacking or challenging documents aren't quite enough, where there's someone who's trying to take advantage of a situation ... more going to the creation of the document and how they've been handled by the fiduciary, maybe unduly influenced, or challenged in some way.*[2]

1.2 Family office conflicts

An increasing number of disputes will likely involve family offices. A family office is a privately held company that typically handles investment management, wealth management and related services for a wealthy family.[3] The family office can be a significant area of contention for fiduciaries, because it may seek to shield the principal and other family members from third-party service providers, including professional trustees. Conflict can arise when the family office treats trustees as transactional or commoditised service providers, limiting the trustees' access to information that they need.[4] For example, a family office may generate disputes when it works on a transaction with its legal and accounting teams and then sends documents relating to the transaction to the trustee, expecting robot-like execution of the documents. A trustee generally needs sufficient information to enable them to make an informed decision that a proposed transaction is copacetic, and that signing the documents is consistent with their fiduciary duties. To do otherwise presents a risk for the trustee, should issues with the transaction arise and litigation ensue. Where fiduciaries are not communicating with the principal directly, they still need a solid sense of what the principal is trying to achieve.

1.3 Compliance-driven conflict, litigation and court activity

We may also be seeing an emerging trend. For offshore trusts, compliance is currently driving litigation and court activity – a trend that has been fuelled by increased pressure on various jurisdictions to improve protections against money laundering. In the Channel Islands, for example, a lawyer's letter is no longer an acceptable means of verifying an individual's residency, according to London-based trust litigator Nick Holland.[5] The net result is that court action is required to free up funds that have been essentially frozen into their existing structures. In the Channel Islands, this often means having to establish the provenance of all the funds in the trust:

> *If the trust is old, that becomes hugely problematic. Some of these trusts are a hundred years old. Trying to prove the source of funds back 100 years ago and then track through any additions that may have taken place to the structure over the 100 years – again, enormous and the burden of proof is on the innocent person whose funds are now being held. It's an enormous amount of work. So, you're basically doing an enormous audit of the entire financial history of these structures and putting it in a format that you can present to the court and [ask that they be] freed up. The cost attendant with tracing back the source of funds can total hundreds of thousands of pounds to complete.*[6]

Similarly, in England, there has been a recent surge in matters involving unexplained wealth orders, which effectively require certain persons to prove the legitimacy of their wealth.[7]

Circumstances like these – where far-reaching compliance obligations dramatically affect innocent beneficiaries and legitimate trust structures – can frustrate a trust's purposes, preventing the trust officials (trustees, trust advisers, protectors and enforcers) from making distributions to those beneficiaries or otherwise using trust property for their benefit. This can anger the beneficiaries, who understandably may question whether the trust officials maintained appropriate records, adequately anticipated new compliance obligations, and properly managed these obligations. Discontent amongst the beneficiaries is magnified when trust assets are tapped to pay the costs associated with addressing these compliance issues.[8] When beneficiaries are disgruntled, disputes tend to follow.[9]

2. Common causes of trust disputes

Fires need three things to start: a source of ignition, a source of fuel, and oxygen. While time may transform their order of significance – or even alter their precise nature – certain core causes spark and feed much of trust litigation:

- poor drafting;
- communication failures;
- lack of education;
- disenfranchisement;
- appointment of the wrong trust officials;
- diminished capacity; and
- challenges of recollection.

All provide the elements necessary to ignite protracted, costly and emotionally damaging trust disputes.

2.1 Poor drafting

A poorly drafted trust instrument can frustrate the settlor's wishes and intent, complicate the trust's administration and trigger or exacerbate disputes. A well-designed, well-drafted trust instrument ideally contains a clear and complete expression of the settlor's wishes and intent. It is a cogent guide that helps to frame a set of shared expectations for trust officials and beneficiaries and it creates a foundation for a good working relationship amongst and between those involved with the trust. When trust officials and beneficiaries have shared expectations, they are less likely to follow a course that leads to disputes.

In contrast, vagueness and ambiguity in a trust instrument create conditions in which disputes more easily arise. A poorly drafted trust instrument does not inevitably produce disputes – a functional group of individuals can overcome the weaknesses in any document – but it can be a catalyst.

While the commodification of trusts – and, here in particular, the commodification of trust creation – has helped to make trusts available to more people, it poses its own perils. Many drafting lawyers use form language to draft trust instruments for their clients. On the one hand, this can make the drafting process more efficient and, in turn, help to contain the fees that clients incur when creating trusts. On the other hand, the use of form language is fraught with a myriad of potential dangers. Some drafting lawyers overreach, relying on forms to create trusts when they do not know or understand the relevant tax and legal issues, or even which trust officials serve which roles and why. For these lawyers, forms substitute for substantive knowledge. They rely too heavily on their own prior form language

"Fires need three things to start: a source of ignition, a source of fuel, and oxygen."

and structure, without critical analysis to make certain the language they use remains effective. Some drafting lawyers cut and paste from various sources, creating a Frankenstein trust instrument that is riddled with errors and internal inconsistencies. The dangers of using form language can also manifest more subtly. Forms can lull drafting lawyers into crafting trusts that do not fully or accurately reflect settlors' wishes and intent.

Of course, overuse of form language is not limited to lawyers. Some institutional trustees have a similar addiction – often insisting upon the inclusion of their own 'standard' language in a trust instrument, even when its inclusion would be redundant given terms already incorporated into the trust by the drafting lawyer. Redundant provisions are rarely worded identically. A good trust litigator will pick them apart and exploit inconsistencies between the two, if a dispute later arises. While not all clients need – or are willing to pay for – personalisation of their trust instruments, it is this personalisation and tailoring of the trust instrument to the specific needs of the situation that can ensure that a trust instrument captures what the settlor wants.

Poor drafting also manifests itself in overly long and frequently unwieldy trust instruments.[10] This undermines readability and understandability. As the trust instrument's length increases, it becomes harder for readers – settlors, beneficiaries, trust officials, lawyers and judges – to understand fully all of the provisions and how the trust works. The likelihood of internal inconsistencies also increases. "People over-build trust documents," according to New York-based estate planning lawyer Rashad Wareh, of Kozusko Harris Duncan.[11] An overly long trust instrument, he says, often contains a litany of procedures that trust officials must follow, and this sets them up for failure:

> *What both leads [to] litigation and might also harm how litigation [proceeds] is that there's too much policies or procedures. There's too much of the kitchen sink in the trust document.*[12]

2.2 Communication failures

With trusts (as with many things), a lack of communication can breed disappointment or discontent. Those emotions, in turn, can lead to disputes. When using a trust to structure wealth, a settlor can often head off problems by communicating the settlor's plans and the thinking behind those plans. This is especially true when a parent is designing a plan that may not otherwise align with the children's expectations. Dealing with dashed expectations can make grieving all the harder and more painful.

The following case, in which one of the co-authors was involved, illustrates this point:

Case history: communication failure

A successful entrepreneur created a trust for the benefit of his two children, both of whom were involved in the family business. He designed the trust so that, upon his death, his daughter would effectively control the business. He did not tell his children. When he died, his son was surprised to learn that his sister would be running the business. The son challenged his father's trust, and acrimonious litigation ensued. The daughter eventually bought him out, but the situation created a deep rift between the siblings. It was not the legacy that their father would have wanted. While there is no certainty that things would have been different, he might have avoided the rancour by explaining to his children his plans and why he felt that those plans made sense. He would also have had an opportunity to listen to his son's concerns and perhaps adjust his plans in a way that may have helped to allay them.

It is not only settlors who should communicate. Many disputes arise because trustees and other trust officials fail to communicate. Communication creates transparency. Transparency fosters trust. Conversely, a lack of communication – a lack of transparency – breeds distrust. When trust officials withhold information – whether it's about the existence of the trust or the activities in which the trust officials are engaged – beneficiaries understandably wonder what they are hiding. Suspicion fills the void. In some cases, beneficiaries perceive the trust officials' reticence to provide information as a manifestation of their arrogance. Sometimes, this perception accurately reflects the trust officials' attitudes; sometimes it does not. The trust instrument may stifle the trust officials' ability to administer the trust in a transparent manner. This may be a flaw in the trust design. In trusts where the trust officials are not restrained from communicating with the beneficiaries, however, open communication generally helps to build rapport and reduce the potential for disputes.[13]

2.3 Lack of education

In some cases, troubles with trusts stem from younger generations lacking an understanding of what it means to be wealthy. They may fail to understand the role that trusts play with respect to family wealth, and how those trusts work. The more senior generations – and, to the extent permitted, the trust officials – can help resolve this by educating the younger generations about wealth and wealth structures. Removing the shroud of mystery and dispelling myths and misconceptions can have a far-reaching impact, heading off potential disputes.

"With trusts (as with many things), a lack of communication can breed disappointment or discontent."

2.4 Disenfranchisement

When beneficiaries don't have a meaningful voice in a trust's administration, they may more easily become frustrated with the trust officials and their administration of the trust. They may feel that they don't have any control, which can exacerbate ill feelings when things are not going as well or as smoothly as they could. Disenfranchisement breeds discontent. In contrast, when they can participate in aspects of decision making or remove and appoint trust officials – or at least influence their removal and appointment – they are more likely to feel that they have some level of voice or control. This empowerment may help to avoid disputes.[14] According to Rashad Wareh, "forcing people to feel like they're on the outside is absolutely a driver of disputes". He offers an example, below, that illustrates this point.

Case history: disenfranchisement

Many years ago, a father created a trust for his son's benefit. The son is a mature, well-functioning adult with his own family but doesn't have any voice in the trust's administration. He has effectively been disenfranchised:

> *There's no family participation at the management level. There's no ability for the family to even have [the fiduciaries] removed and [replaced by] some independent person who qualifies under a certain criterion, a large bank for example. Even that limited flexibility isn't there ... What's been created is [a situation in which the beneficiary] has a very antagonistic relationship with the [trustee] ... It's not a healthy relationship.*[15]

2.5 Appointment of the wrong trust officials

With trusts, the governance structure can be as simple as having one trustee, or it may be complex, involving multiple trust officials – trustees, trust advisers, protectors and enforcers – and potentially even different classes of trust officials. Whether the governance structure is simple or complex, having the wrong trust officials can create or exacerbate trust disputes. A person can be wrong for the role of trust official for any number of reasons, as below.

Skills deficit: A person may lack the skill, experience or knowledge to serve in the role. Sometimes, this is because the trust's complexity outstrips the trust official's competency – irrespective of whether the trust official is an individual, bank or trust company. Trusts vary in their complexity for myriad reasons. Complexity can be a function of the settlor's intent, the family's situation or a tax objective. It can be a function of the assets that the trust holds. A trust that holds a significant interest in an operating company typically involves more complexity than a trust that holds a modest portfolio of publicly traded securities, for example. In some cases, a trust's complexity

"Disenfranchisement breeds discontent. In contrast, when [beneficiaries] can participate in aspects of decision making or remove and appoint trust officials – or at least influence their removal and appointment – they are more likely to feel that they have some level of voice or control."

is a function of the settlor's penchant for complexity. Other times, a trust becomes complex after the wrong person is appointed at the trust's inception. Trusts evolve as family circumstances and assets change. Trusts can outgrow their trust officials and a person who was right at one point in time may no longer be right later on.

Bias: Bias can also compromise a person's fit for an official role with a trust. An individual may have a conscious bias (sometimes called an explicit bias) or an unconscious bias (sometimes called an implicit bias). Either way, the bias may affect the person's decision making, potentially causing them to administer the trust in a way that is contrary to the settlor's intent. For example, the terms of the trust may envision that the trustee will make distributions to the settlor's children, maintaining them in the standard of living to which the settlor was accustomed. An individual trustee who grew up in a working-class family may have fixed personal views concerning expenditures for goods and travel that differ from the settlor's views. An expenditure one person considers to be a luxury may not be viewed as such by someone else.

If an individual allows personal bias to influence decisions concerning distributions to the settlor's children, they may be ill-suited to serve as trustee. Banks and trust companies often try to mitigate bias by using

"A good lawyer understands trusts, has experience with their administration, and often develops a good understanding of the settlor and the settlor's family, which can inform the administration of the trust."

committees or other multi-person decision-making processes. These processes are effective to a degree, but their efficacy has limits, especially when the decision makers are homogeneous or lack diverse perspective, or when the peer-review structure tacitly encourages decision makers to acquiesce to one another (or to one alpha member).

Conflict: A person may also be wrong for the role of trust official because of a conflict of interests. A trust official's personal interests may conflict with those of the beneficiaries – particularly in the investment context. A trustee may have a personal or proprietary interest in which they wish to invest trust property, for example a company founded by the trustee in a personal capacity. Many trust instruments waive this type of conflict, although it is increasingly common to see processes by which a trust official must disclose, and obtain approval for, any transaction that may be a conflict.

A conflict also may arise by reason of the roles that the trust official plays. All too often, a drafting lawyer prepares a trust instrument that appoints the lawyer as a trustee. Is the settlor's estate planning representative the right person to serve as trustee? Are the best interests of the trust served by such an appointment? Maybe. Or maybe not. Experienced trust litigators view such appointments as a potential red flag, warranting a deeper look.

A good lawyer understands trusts, has experience with their administration, and often develops a good understanding of the settlor and the settlor's family, which can inform the administration of the trust. A drafting lawyer, however, also faces potential competing interests when serving as a trustee. The lawyer owes a duty to the settlor and has an economic interest in keeping the settlor happy as a client, which may incline them to administer the trust as the settlor directs even though that may not be consistent with the terms of the trust. The lawyer may tend to act as the settlor's alter ego. The lawyer may also be reluctant to acknowledge or fix potential problems that arise with the trust or its administration – such as an ambiguity in the terms of the trust or other flaws in the trust's design – because that may mean acknowledging their own mistakes. These same advantages and disadvantages potentially apply when a drafting lawyer serves as a protector or in any other role within a trust's governance structure.

All these factors highlight the importance of careful planning when selecting trust officials.

2.6 Diminished capacity (including undue influence)
Whether an individual has the legally sufficient mental capacity to execute documents and authorise transactions is a common and critical focus of litigation. It is also a question that can pose significant evidentiary challenges. When a dispute over capacity arises, litigators may be called upon to try to prove the existence (or diminution) of cognitive ability with precision years after the event in question, using witnesses who often prove ill-equipped for the task. Implementing measures to affirm capacity at critical moments such as the execution of a trust document can meaningfully alleviate that burden.

Profiling diminishing capacity as exclusively an issue for the elderly brings considerable risk. One of the primary reasons often cited for the recent increase in trust litigation against fiduciaries is the shift in population as the generation born immediately following World War II retires.[16] Cognitive diminution and weakened intellect may traditionally be more evident in an ageing cohort. If the concern is characterised solely as generational, however, it can become all too easy to default to the belief that the implementation of measures specifically directed to affirming a settlor's capacity are only required when the elderly are involved. The issue is broader than that. For those characterising the issue of capacity as directed solely at an ageing population, cautionary tales increasingly abound.

Advances in medicine have not only prolonged life expectancy but also led to more frequent detection of diseases and conditions impacting cognitive abilities much earlier in the human lifespan than even a decade ago. Modern diagnoses like early-onset or 'probable' dementia or Alzheimer's are not limited to the boomer generation. The increasingly early detection of such conditions in the younger population presents significant evidentiary challenges. Barring a traumatic event, cognitive decline is gradual and marked with significant periods of fluidity. The challenge lies in:

- truing up whether capacity exists in the present moment, for an individual so diagnosed; and
- when looking backwards, ascertaining whether capacity existed at a specific moment in the continuum of cognitive decline.

A recent case involving one of the co-authors illustrates the point:

Case history: capacity

A 45-year-old woman was diagnosed with probable Alzheimer's disease in 2013. This diagnosis was made by a neurologist approximately nine months after a routine annual examination by the woman's primary care physician. During that annual exam, the woman made idle conversation with her doctor about recent movie releases and struggled to recall the name of her favourite actor. An offhand, joking remark to her physician about "everything falling apart" now that she had turned 45 ultimately led to the proactive neurology referral.

Disputes subsequently arose over certain financial and estate planning decisions made by the woman in an eight-year period surrounding the date of her diagnosis. The central issues focused on when the woman's cognitive abilities began to decline and to what extent they were compromised at the moment the contested decisions were made. No proactive measures were taken to confirm the woman's cognitive abilities at any moment in time relevant to the disputed decisions. Capacity had to be established retrospectively, leaning on three common sources of evidence in matters involving capacity:

- medical providers;
- lay witnesses – eg, family members; and (to a lesser extent)
- the woman's recent care providers.

None of that evidence provided a clear answer to either of the two central questions.

Medical evidence and testimony from care givers can be helpful but tends to be incapable of time-stamping cognitive ability with precision. In this case, the formal diagnosis provided an indication that the decline had commenced as of the date of diagnosis, but the woman's neurologist was unable to reliably estimate when the decline began in earnest or how far into the progression of the disease she was at that time.[17] Friends and family members typically have their own set of challenges in ascertaining whether a loved one has capacity.[18] Such was the case here. Multiple witnesses reflected on whether and when they first noticed signs of any cognitive decline. Unsurprisingly, conclusions varied. Several offered distinctly different recollections of the exact same experiences with the woman. Others summarily concluded the diagnosis must be inaccurate – a position they continued to maintain, years later, despite clear signs to the contrary. In the end, the only consensus they were able to reach was that the decline appeared to be gradual and not a dramatic fall-off. The woman continued to have at least moments or periods of meaningful cognitive ability for an extended time after her diagnosis – none of which helped effectively establish whether she had capacity to make the decisions at issue some ten years prior.

Minimising the potential for trust disputes involving capacity means implementing protocols at the outset that can provide evidence of capacity at seminal moments for the trust and trust administration.

Practitioners (and the trust) are better served if the lawyer takes detailed notes of their interactions with the client, documenting the

"Minimising the potential for trust disputes involving capacity means implementing protocols at the outset that can provide evidence of capacity at seminal moments for the trust and trust administration."

elements of testamentary capacity – including the client's understanding of the nature and extent of their wealth, which are two of the more difficult elements to establish.

2.7 Challenges of recollection

In practice, relying on the lawyer, or a witness to the execution of the trust deed, to support a trust from challenge is something of a fallacy. Neither may recall any of the specifics.

Case history: imperfect recall

At a deposition in the autumn of 2021, a third-party client was subpoenaed to answer a series of questions about estate documents she witnessed her deceased mother execute nearly 25 years earlier. The witness had no recollection of ever seeing the document, let alone the circumstances surrounding its execution or substantive discussions about the underlying estate plan.

Substantial time lapses are common, as are a witness' minimal (or non-existent) recollection of the execution conference. Standardising a protocol that documents a settlor's mental and testamentary capacity at the critical moments in the trust's development strengthens the trust from challenge and can dissuade capacity claims altogether. It is much easier to establish capacity in real time than to attempt to reconstruct its existence years later.

3. Our approach

What can you do to reduce the risk of a trust dispute? Quite a lot, actually. Over the next four chapters we explore ideas for avoiding trust disputes during each phase of a trust's lifecycle:

- design;
- execution;
- administration; and
- termination.

II. Trust dispute avoidance through design

Good trust design can help to pre-empt disputes. Even before a settlor creates a trust, there is much that can be done to reduce the potential for disputes. There are a number of ways in which trust design can help:

- managing the settlor's expectations;
- good drafting;
- creating the appropriate governance structure;
- communicating with the beneficiaries;
- incorporating flexibility and adaptability;
- selecting appropriate liability and evidentiary standards;
- using a no-contest or forfeiture provision;
- incorporating processes for non-judicial dispute resolution; and
- getting the litigator's perspective early.

We will examine each of these. As we do, you will see that a theme emerges: proactively engaging with the beneficiaries often plays an invaluable preventative role.

1. Managing the settlor's expectations

An important step in designing trusts is helping the settlor understand how they work, what their limitations are, and how things can go awry. The lawyers and other advisers who work with settlors can play a key role in this. Some settlors have prior experience with trusts. They may have been beneficiaries of trusts created by their parents, grandparents or others. Or they may have created trusts themselves. Some of them have a good understanding of trusts, while others may have only a superficial understanding. Some settlors lack any prior experience with trusts. They may be unfamiliar with the concept, the terminology, and who plays which roles with respect to a trust. For them, this educational process may be more involved. Either way, having a good understanding of trusts helps settlors acquire more realistic expectations about how they function and what they can achieve.

Using trusts, some settlors seek to exert significant control over the beneficiaries' behaviour or the management of property held in trust. They may seek to encourage – or even dictate – certain choices concerning employment, marriage and religious practices. Although jurisdictions vary in the degree to which they tolerate this, settlors can generally impose significant control. And whether implementing such controls is wise is a separate question entirely. If they are well conceived and executed, certain controls might have a laudable effect; if not, they potentially create a climate ripe for disputes. If the beneficiaries do not share the values underpinning the controls, one or more of them may bristle at the controls and even openly challenge the restrictive terms of the trust.

In some cases, drafting an effective trust under such circumstances is a matter of striking the right note: finding a balance between the settlor's desire for control, and dispute mitigation. By giving up some control, a settlor paradoxically may be more likely to achieve their wishes and objectives, encouraging the beneficiaries to embrace the trust and helping to lessen the potential for disputes. This result may be even more likely if combined with an ongoing programme to educate the beneficiaries about wealth and the role that trusts play.

2. Good drafting

Good drafting is fundamental to avoiding disputes. A trust instrument should articulate the settlor's intent and wishes clearly, in a manner that is both accessible to the reader and not susceptible to misinterpretation.[19] As Warren Buffett has observed, stilted jargon and complex constructions are usually the culprits when a well-intentioned, informed writer fails to get the message across to an intelligent, interested reader.[20]

Writing in plain English is crucial. The best writing breaks concepts down into separate, easily digestible parts. Short, simple sentences are better than long, complex ones.[21] Short paragraphs are better than long paragraphs. The best writing uses words and phrases that

"[D]rafting lawyers [should] spend more time thinking about three things: clarity, readability and flexibility."

have a precise, consistent meaning. Good drafting eschews words that are potentially ambiguous, even though some have been staples of legal drafting. For example, the words, 'shall', 'herein', 'hereunder', 'thereof' and 'notwithstanding', and the conjunctive-disjunctive 'and/or' do not have consistent meanings, can create confusion, and thus should be avoided.[22]

As part of his practice, Rashad Wareh reviews a significant number of trust documents written by lawyers outside his law firm. "My biggest critique," he says, "is that they are written for the professionals and *not* the clients and *not* the beneficiaries."[23] He recommends that drafting lawyers spend more time thinking about three things: clarity, readability and flexibility.

> *What could [drafters] improve? Readability of the document, thinking of the family and the beneficiaries as the primary readers. Because all of us professionals and the institutions, I would hope, can understand that document, no matter how it's written. It might be painful, but they could do it. But who's the real audience here? And make sure you clearly express [the settlor's] intentions. Letters of wishes are useful ... in giving further guidance after the trust has been created. But too few [drafters] build that guidance into the document. [Second], try to write flexibly. Try to give people some*

> *form of ownership and control within the limits of the [settlor's] wishes.*[24]

Beyond the wording itself, orientation of provisions within the trust document can detract from clarity. Does their orientation lend itself to readability and clarity for lay people – the clients and the beneficiaries? In our interview, Rashad provided recent examples where his firm was engaged to review and provide a second opinion on core estate planning documents prepared by other firms. In each, the actual trust provisions were buried toward the back of 20- and 30-page trust instruments, behind layers of language on purely administrative topics. That structure presents a common problem. Until the reader reaches the end of the document, the identity of the beneficiaries, how distributions can be made for them, and whether they possess any powers of their own, such as powers of appointment, can be entirely unclear. When it comes to disputes, readability matters.

Thoughtful simplicity is another hallmark of good drafting. Although some trust instruments are underdeveloped, a more common problem is the unwieldy, over-engineered trust instrument. Overly lengthy documents undermine readability and understandability, are more likely to contain internal inconsistencies, and are more likely to set trust officials up to fail. Rashad offers some advice for drafters:

"Thoughtful simplicity is another hallmark of good drafting. Although some trust instruments are underdeveloped, a more common problem is the unwieldy, over-engineered trust instrument."

I think for a variety of reasons – whether it's from the trustee's perspective or the attorney's perspective – don't over-build the trust.

3. Creating the appropriate governance structure

A well-designed governance structure will mitigate the risk of disputes. First, it establishes the roles for governing the trust and allocates powers and duties among the roles in a manner that is appropriate to the complexity of the trust, the dispositive terms and the scope and type of property that it holds.[25] Secondly, it establishes a set of checks and balances, so that each trust official (ie, trustee, trust adviser, protector or enforcer) is accountable for their conduct – for example, a trust instrument should generally include mechanisms for removing a trust official and appointing a successor. Thirdly, it establishes rules that help to ensure that each trust official is well qualified for the role. Through qualification standards and appointment processes, a trust instrument should aim to ensure that each trust official has the skill and experience suitable to the role that the trust official plays within the trust. And fourthly, it establishes an appropriate standard – fiduciary or non-fiduciary – to which the person will be subject in the performance of their duties.

3.1 Checks and balances

A thoughtful system of checks and balances helps to keep trust officials accountable, facilitate the transition from trust officials to their successors, and potentially reduce the likelihood of disputes. There are four elements of a good system of checks and balances, as follows.

(a) Non-judicial processes for appointment, resignation and removal

The trust instrument should establish processes for the appointment, resignation and removal of trust officials, without the need to go to court.

The objective here is to establish self-contained, continuous, non-judicial processes for the oversight and succession of trust officials. The processes for appointing and removing trust officials should not contain any gaps – temporal or otherwise. In the past, many trust instruments did not contain any trustee removal provisions. The net result generally locked the initial trustees into their role in perpetuity, absent a serious breach of trust and the beneficiaries' resolve to pursue legal action. Thankfully, this is now less common (though, regrettably, it seems most common when the drafting lawyer is the initial trustee). Some trust instruments, however, do not address even reasonably anticipated contingencies.

Case history: successor trustees
In a recent matter involving one of the co-authors, a settlor established a revocable trust in which she (as initial trustee) named specific individuals to serve as successor co-trustees for the revocable trust itself, when she no longer had the capacity to serve, as well as separate successor co-trustees for sub-trusts created under the trust when it became irrevocable. Unfortunately, the trust was silent as to the appointment of successors. While trustees were allowed to resign at any time, it contained no provision, criteria or qualification standard for the appointment of successor co-trustees and no mechanism for the appointment of successors. This was true of the sub-trusts as well, even though each of them was designed to serve younger generation descendants. When the successor trustees all sought to resign at once, the trust provided no guidance as to their successors. Failure to anticipate such a simple contingency led to conflict and costly litigation.

Other avoidable examples are readily available. A trust instrument may provide that the settlor has the power to remove a trust official but fail to address what happens if the settlor becomes incapacitated or what happens after the settlor's death. It may provide that a majority of the beneficiaries who have attained 21 years of age may remove a trust official, but fail to address what happens if all of the beneficiaries are younger than that.[26] Similarly, it may allow a majority of a class of beneficiaries to remove a trust official while concurrently defining the class in a way in which the class may not actually have any members. This sometimes happens in a trust designed as a US trust for US tax purposes. The trust instrument may exclude a non-US person from the class of persons who can appoint or remove a trust official.

(b) Vested interest provisions
A person who has the power to remove a trustee or other trust official should generally not have an interest in whether the trust official continues to serve. If the personal interests of the person holding the removal power may be enhanced by refraining from exercising the removal power, there is an incentive to leave in place a trust official who may be ill-suited (or worse) for the role. For example, some trust instruments provide that a majority of the trustees may remove a trustee. This can foster in-group bias, in which the trustees exhibit favouritism toward their fellow trustees. A trustee may be less likely to speak out against another trustee, because doing so may increase the risk of someone speaking out against them. The hazard of personal interests eroding the checks and balances may be even more acute when the drafting lawyer is the trustee and the drafting lawyer's partners (or a subset of the partners) have the power to remove a trustee. The partners may have little incentive to upset the status quo – and the revenue stream – potentially locking in the drafting lawyer as

trustee. A more thoughtful and generally more effective approach would be to empower someone who has no personal stake in whether a particular person is trustee with the power to remove any incumbent.

(c) Familiarity with the provisions of the trust

A person who has the power to remove a trustee or other trust official needs to know about the trust and its administration. This may seem obvious, but a trust instrument that modifies or waives the duty to inform may render a person holding a removal power ignorant of circumstances that would warrant the trust official's removal. A lack of information can neutralise this important check and balance. Consider, for example, a trust instrument wherein the settlor gives the beneficiaries the power to remove a trustee but imposes no duty on the trustee to inform the beneficiaries about the trust's existence or any aspect of its administration. In that trust, the removal power is effectively meaningless. The trust instrument should require the trust officials to keep key people informed about the trust and its administration. Those people may be the beneficiaries, their proxies (so long as the proxies have an incentive to act in the beneficiaries' interests) or the persons holding the removal power. If the beneficiaries or their proxies do not have the removal power but are dissatisfied with a trust official's conduct, they certainly have an incentive to persuade the persons who do hold the removal power to exercise the power and remove that trust official.

(d) Incentive to act in beneficiaries' interests

A person who has the power to appoint a trustee or other trust official should be incentivised to act in the beneficiaries' interests. If the beneficiaries have the appointment power, their self-interest is adequate incentive. This does not mean that they will always make the right choice, though – a primary reason why empowering beneficiaries to appoint trust officials is not always the wisest course. Some beneficiaries lack the maturity – financial or otherwise – to make sound decisions concerning who is well suited to serve as a trust official, while others with addictive behaviours such as substance abuse or gambling might be motivated to pick trust officials who would administer the trust in a manner contrary to their best interests. Of course, there is much to be said for educating beneficiaries about wealth and helping them manage any deleterious behaviours so that they can have an effective voice in a trust for their benefit. If, however, someone other than the beneficiaries has the power of appointment, what incentive do they have to act in the beneficiaries' interests?

For example, if a protector (in the United States, more commonly a 'trust protector') has the power to appoint a trustee, what incentive does the protector have to exercise the power in furtherance of the beneficiaries' interests? Perhaps little or none. The trust instrument should address this. Although some trust instruments provide that a protector does not hold the power to appoint a trust official in a non-fiduciary capacity (or, even more broadly, is not a fiduciary), a better approach might be to impose a fiduciary duty on the protector's exercise of the power. When the protector has a fiduciary duty to act in the beneficiaries' best interests when appointing a trust official, the protector will have an incentive to exercise the power thoughtfully. Otherwise, the protector risks personal liability. Drafting lawyers – especially since they may serve as protectors – are not always receptive to this approach.[27]

3.2 Selecting the right person for each role

The risk of a dispute is mitigated by making certain the right person occupies the right role for a given trust. Simply stated, a person who is well suited to a given role is more likely to act appropriately and avoid problems. A person who is ill-fitted for a role is more likely to act inappropriately (whether intentionally or unintentionally) and create problems. Whether it is the settlor selecting the initial trust officials or someone else appointing an additional or successor trust official, the imperative is the same – choose wisely.[28] An array of persons can serve as trust officials: individuals, institutions large and small, professionals and non-professionals. There are advantages and disadvantages with each, and these should be carefully considered at the design and creation stage.

(a) Non-professional individuals (family members, friends etc)

A non-professional individual, such as a family member, friend or business partner, is typically selected because they have intimate knowledge of the settlor's values and wishes, as well as the family's situation and dynamics. That knowledge can inform decisions concerning distributions, investments and other matters affecting the trust. A non-professional individual, however, may not know how to properly administer a trust, leading to breaches of trust or other problems. They may also be more susceptible to making decisions based on personal emotion or bias. Additionally, with any individual serving as a trust official, apathy, incapacity or death will affect their ability to serve. Of course, good advisers can mitigate that risk – but care must be exercised in selecting advisers properly suited to the task.

(b) Professional individuals (lawyers, etc)

A professional individual, like a lawyer, accountant or investment adviser, can often provide highly attentive and personal service. While they tend to have specialised knowledge in a given field, professionals may have limited skills in others. For example, a lawyer may not be as skilled in managing an investment portfolio as an investment professional. Similarly, some professional individuals have

"The risk of a dispute is mitigated by making certain the right person occupies the right role for a given trust."

an in-depth understanding of trust administration, while others do not. A business lawyer who serves as trustee for clients may be well versed in mergers and acquisitions while lacking an understanding of the laws governing trust investments and fiduciary duties (and may be more susceptible to making decisions based on his client's directions than the terms of the trust). In some cases, professional individuals work within a firm that provides a suite of trust-related services, complementing their skills and enabling them to administer a trust more fully and effectively.

(c) Small institutions

A small institution may offer attentive, personal service but tends to offer a more limited array of services. Further, it can often lack the sophistication to handle more complicated trust structures or investment portfolios. An institutional trustee can provide more continuity than an individual trustee, although staffing changes can affect the quality of the institution's service. For matters affecting a trust, an institutional trustee also generally makes decisions by committee or by at least two individuals. Although this more bureaucratic process may be slower than with an individual acting alone, it can reduce the risk of cognitive and emotional biases. A small institution may also be susceptible to acquisition by a larger institution, which can presage changes in scope, nature and cost of the service that it provides.

(d) Large institutions
In contrast to a small institution, larger institutions may offer more sophisticated services, or at least a broader suite of services. As with any institution, a large entity may experience staff turnover, which can erode personal connections with the family and institutional knowledge about the trust. A large institution may also be more likely to implement risk management policies that apply without exception across all trust relationships, forcing out trust structures that do not conform to its established set of rules for permissible arrangements. This is evidenced by many large institutions eschewing trusts that hold interests in family businesses, for example. Experience has shown that a large institution may also be more likely to de-risk or otherwise abandon trust services as a business line, which can leave trust officials and beneficiaries scrambling for a suitable replacement.

(e) Special purpose entities
In the context of trust governance structures, a special purpose entity is an entity that serves as a trust official. Typically, the role served is discrete from that of trustee – such as distribution director, investment director or protector – which allows the entity to avoid the licensing obligations to which it would be subject if it served as a trustee. It generally offers a way for individuals to participate in a trust's administration – say by making decisions concerning distributions or investments – while avoiding some of the downsides of individuals personally serving as trust officials.

A special purpose entity potentially offers a few advantages:

- It may help to shield the individual decision makers – ie, the entity's directors or managers – from liability arising from the trust's administration. This may make it more attractive for a skilled, experienced individual to participate in a trust's administration, because it helps to insulate the individual from personal liability. This protection, however, may be ephemeral if the entity is not adequately capitalised or does not maintain adequate errors and omissions insurance.
- It may help to minimise jurisdictional risks. When an individual serves as a trust official, the courts in the jurisdiction in which that individual resides may have jurisdiction over the trust. That may create a risk that the settlor's intent will be less fully respected – or perhaps even defeated – or that the trust property will be exposed to third-party claims. That jurisdiction's laws and courts may exhibit different attitudes toward trusts than the preferred forum for disputes involving the trust. (The preferred forum typically would be the jurisdiction in which the trust's principal place of administration is located.) By using a special purpose entity, an individual can potentially participate

in decision making with respect to the trust without creating those jurisdictional risks. Of course, it is important that the entity avoid becoming subject to the jurisdiction outside the preferred forum, which may require the entity's key decisions to be made in the preferred forum or at least another favourable jurisdiction.

- It may help to minimise the taxes to which the trust is subject. Specifically, it might avoid causing the trust to have nexus in a jurisdiction that taxes a trust based on the residency of a fiduciary of the trust. An individual who is a resident of such a jurisdiction could potentially serve as a director or manager of a special purpose entity formed in the preferred forum. Of course, it is important that the entity avoid creating nexus in another jurisdiction. Thus, the entity should avoid conducting activities where there may be unfavourable tax implications for the trust. This generally means that the entity's directors or managers must conduct their activities outside any tax-sensitive jurisdictions.
- Importantly, a special purpose entity may help to formalise the succession process. When an individual personally serves as a trust official, it can be more challenging to identify potential successors, develop them, and transition the decision making smoothly to them. Although a trust could accomplish this through a committee structure, an entity can potentially facilitate succession more readily and be positioned to adjust more easily to changing circumstances and objectives. It's often easier to modify or vary the terms of the entity's governing documents than the terms of a trust.

(f) Private trust companies

A private trust company is a legal entity that typically provides trust services to one family.[29] It may be licensed or unlicensed. A licensed private trust company obtains a licence or charter from a banking regulator, which supervises the company's activities on an ongoing basis. An unlicensed private trust company is exempt from any licensing or chartering obligation but generally must comply with certain requirements governing its organisation and operation. For some wealthy families, a private trust company marries the most attractive qualities of individual trustees and commercial institutional trustees. It can provide bespoke, professional trust services that the family controls.

For a family that already has a family office, a private trust company can be especially attractive, as it can provide control, attentiveness and a personalised service. Generally, a family can mould a private trust company to its needs and circumstances. Although a private trust company provides continuity as trustee, succession planning within the private trust company is critical. Of principal concern is that the private trust company needs to develop and retain talent. For a family that does not already have a family office or is not already working together in a family business, a private trust company can be a bit daunting, because the family is internalising certain responsibilities for what essentially is a family-run business focusing on managing the family's trusts.

(g) Using a blended structure

A trust's governance structure is often more effective when it includes a diverse group of decision makers. Incorporating both professionals and non-professionals into the governance structure can help to ensure well-informed decisions from both a legal perspective (ie, how to administer the trust in compliance with the terms of the trust and relevant legal obligations) and a family perspective (ie, how to take account of the wants, needs, concerns and circumstances of the family members and other beneficiaries). Professionals generally and unsurprisingly have more skill and experience in the proper technical administration of trusts than non-professionals. But the potential value add in having a non-professional in the mix can be quite significant. Blending professionals and non-professionals – which can be as simple as a trust company and a beneficiary as co-trustees or a

"Incorporating both professionals and non-professionals into the governance structure can help to ensure well-informed decisions from both a legal perspective and a family perspective."

complex structure involving a trustee, protector and other trust officials – can create an inherent system of checks and balances that fosters sound trust administration.

Professionals can help steer governance clear of mistakes that give rise to disputes and other problems. Some non-professional fiduciaries are not versed in reading trust instruments. Instead of following the terms of the trust, they make distributions to whomever they wish and for whatever purposes they feel is appropriate. Why do they do it? Often, because they simply feel it's right or perhaps because it is what they believe a deceased settlor would have wanted. Consider two examples recently encountered by the co-authors:

Case histories: the pitfalls of non-professional trustees

In the first example, a non-professional trustee distributed trust property to a beneficiary's adult child (ie, the settlor's grandchild) for their enjoyment – even though the terms of the trust only permitted distributions to the beneficiary (the settlor's child) during the beneficiary's lifetime. In the second, a non-professional trustee made direct distributions to two of the trust's beneficiaries – despite express language in the trust mandating that all such distributions be made only through the beneficiaries' respective sub-trusts. Why? Because the trustee believed that the maturity issues that gave cause for creation of the sub-trusts had been (to the trustee's mind) resolved.

In both examples, the non-professional trustees ignored the express terms of the respective trusts for subjective reasons.

A professional co-trustee can potentially avert such trust breaches. Given their skills and experience, professionals are typically more rigorous in adhering to the terms of the trust. They tend to be more attentive to compliance with tax and legal obligations, including any obligations to keep the beneficiaries informed about a trust and its administration. Some are more attuned to how personal biases may influence decision making, and actively seek to avoid any improper influence those biases may have. Professionals are more likely to employ four-eye reviews or committee-based decisions, which can potentially help eradicate any detrimental effect of such biases.

While many, if not most, professional trust officials diligently seek insight into the lives of the beneficiaries – and, in the case of newly settled trusts, the settlors – they rarely attain the depth of knowledge possessed by non-professionals. This may be most obvious in banks and trust companies that serve as trustee for a large number of trusts. A trust officer who is responsible for 200 to 300 trust accounts – which may represent 60 to 150 families – has limited time in which to develop and maintain relationships with the beneficiaries of those trusts. In contrast, non-professional trust officials typically have a much richer knowledge of the beneficiaries and their situations, because they are related to the beneficiaries or have close personal relationships with one or more of them.

3.3 Beneficiary committees

When a certain role in a trust's governance is best held by a beneficiary, it may be advantageous to design the role so that it is held by a committee, rather than by one individual. A beneficiary committee is a way of giving voice to several beneficiaries, whose views can potentially inform the decisions required in the governance structure. Giving people a voice can help to avoid the ill will that can spark trust disputes. This may be especially valuable when a trust benefits several branches of a family, as the committee approach enables each branch to participate in certain decisions. It also can help to temper or avoid the tyranny of one individual – for example, the eldest sibling – over other family members. Incorporating a beneficiary committee into a trust's structure, of course, demands careful attention to qualification and succession issues. For example, who qualifies to serve as a member of the committee? How are members of the committee appointed or elected? What is the process for removing a member of the committee? Is a member of a committee entitled to compensation? Addressing these types of questions helps to ensure the efficient operation of the committee and avoid potential disputes.

3.4 Qualifications

Is a particular person qualified to serve as a trustee or other trust official? In many trusts, settlors at least partially answer that question by specifying the minimum qualifications that a person must have to serve in a given role. Qualifications often aim to ensure that a trust official has a minimum level of experience. For example, a trust instrument might provide that any person who can direct the trust's investments must have at least 10 years of experience in investment management. By their nature, qualifications are exclusionary. They bar certain persons from serving in certain roles. Preventing a beneficiary's ne'er-do-well college roommate from having a say in making distributions from a family's trust is a laudable goal. Query whether qualifications are always – or even usually – the optimal way to achieve such goals.

In some cases, the qualifications are dictated by the desire to have a professional serve in a particular role. If the settlor wishes to have an institutional professional trustee, the trust instrument might provide that the trustee must be a bank or trust company. If the settlor wishes to allow either individual or institutional professional trustees to serve in the role, the trust instrument might provide that the trustee must be a bank, trust company, lawyer or accountant. Sometimes, the qualifications are more granular. For example, the trust instrument may provide that a bank or trust company must serve as trustee of trusts that have a combined value that exceeds a specified threshold (eg, US$500 million). Or the trust instrument may provide that a lawyer serving in the role must have been practising primarily trust and estate law for 10 or more years.

In some cases, a qualification is tax motivated. For example, in the case of a trust that is designed to be a foreign trust for US tax purposes, the trust instrument might require the trustee to be a non-US person. Similarly, in the case of a trust that is created by a US citizen for purposes of keeping the trust property out of their estate for US estate tax purposes, the trust instrument might require the trustee to be a person who, with respect to the settlor, is not a related or subordinate party. These tax-motivated qualifications are usually unavoidable.

As with other aspects of trust design, qualifications should be drafted with care. They exclude certain persons from serving as trustees or other trust officials. If not artfully drafted, they may inadvertently exclude some otherwise qualified persons from serving. Consider the

"Is a particular person qualified to serve as a trustee or other trust official? In many trusts, settlors at least partially answer that question by specifying the minimum qualifications that a person must have to serve in a given role."

"Drafting with care – and with at least one eye watching for possible disputes downstream – is an essential element of trust design."

trust instrument that was governed by the laws of a US state and required a professional trustee to be a 'corporate' trustee. This potentially excluded any bank or trust company that was organised as a limited liability company, because it was not a corporation and thus not a 'corporate' entity. Or consider the trust instrument that required a bank or trust company to have US$500 million of capital. This qualification would exclude many trust companies that do not provide depository services, because they are generally not subject to the same capital requirements as banks. Similarly, a trust instrument that requires a trust company to have a certain level of assets under management would generally exclude any trust company that provides trustee services but does not provide investment management services.

Instead of imposing qualifications (except where necessary to satisfy some tax or other legal requirement), alternatives may be available. For example, the settlor could entrust the persons who have the power to select successor trust officials with the discretion to pick whomever they believe is most well suited for the role. This approach allows greater flexibility, because the selection of successor trust officials is not limited by the qualifications. On the other hand, the approach puts greater reliance on cultivating and maintaining a robust succession process. Doing so likely entails educating the persons who have the appointment powers about wealth and ensuring that they are engaged with the family and the trust's administration. This helps to enable them to make well-informed decisions. In addition, it is important to address any potential conflicts, so that those with appointment powers do not have an incentive to elevate personal interests over the interests of the beneficiaries and the trust's purposes. In many trusts, all of this may not be feasible. Sometimes, it is more practical to impose qualification requirements.

Drafting with care – and with at least one eye watching for possible disputes downstream – is an essential element of trust design.

3.5 Fiduciary versus non-fiduciary capacity

Whether a person holds a power in a fiduciary or non-fiduciary capacity can affect both how the person exercises that power, as well as the degree to which the exercise or non-exercise of the power creates risk of a trust dispute. A trust official can potentially hold and exercise one or more powers in either a fiduciary or non-fiduciary capacity.[30] The primary difference is accountability to the beneficiaries: with fiduciary status, a trust official is potentially more accountable to the beneficiaries, while non-fiduciary status often means less accountability. Accordingly, in designing the governance structure, careful consideration should be given to whether the trust officials will act in a fiduciary or non-fiduciary capacity.

Designating a trust official as a non-fiduciary may have appeal because it can (at least partially) insulate the trust official from liability. But fiduciary status and the attendant liability for breaching fiduciary duties can be an important check on the trust official. Fiduciary status can incentivise the trust official to act prudently and in accordance with the terms of the trust. Such an incentive can reduce the risk of trust disputes.

3.6 Term limits

Although seemingly uncommon, some trust instruments limit the term of trustees or other trust officials. As with term limits generally, the objective is to infuse a trust's governance with new blood – with a fresh perspective and new ideas being potentially very beneficial. Of course, there can be disadvantages, as well. Changing a trustee or other trust official is potentially disruptive. There is a loss of at least some institutional knowledge, even if other trust officials remain in place. The new trust official needs to get up to speed on the terms of the trust, learn about the beneficiaries and their circumstances, and develop constructive working relationships with the other trust officials. Further, absent some other procedures or qualifications that work in concert with the term limit, there is no guarantee that a new person would bring a fresh perspective or new ideas. If the trust limits a trustee's term to 10 years and requires any successor trustee to be a bank or trust company, what's to say that the successor trustee will be any better than its predecessor? In many cases, a periodic review of the trust and its administration by independent specialists may offer more meaningful results than imposing term limits on a trust official.

3.7 Age limits

Some trust instruments impose age limits on individual trustees and other trust officials – either as a prerequisite or a cap to service. As an example of the former, some trust instruments provide that a beneficiary must have attained 30 years of age before serving as a trustee. Although the latter are seemingly less common, some trust instruments impose a mandatory retirement age, forcing an individual trust official to cease serving upon attaining, for example, 75 years of age. Should a trust instrument impose age limits like these?

A minimum age requirement can be intended as a proxy for emotional or financial maturity. Sometimes, it is a proxy for experience. In either case, it is an imperfect proxy. Some 20-somethings are more mature than some 30-somethings (or even 40-somethings). Likewise, by their mid-20s, some individuals have had richer and more diverse experiences – for example, through volunteering, public or military

"A maximum age requirement is often a crude proxy for mental acuity. It presumes that, after a certain age, an individual's mental faculties inexorably decline. In this era of advancing healthcare and longevity, this type of mandatory retirement age has questionable value."

service, or entrepreneurial ventures – than someone who has spent decades as a ski bum or clubber. For some families, a minimum age requirement may be useful despite its imperfections. For other families – especially wealthy ones – a better approach may be to ensure that the next generation has opportunities to learn about what it means to be wealthy and has opportunities to enrich their lives – and the lives of others – through diverse experiences.

A maximum age requirement is often a crude proxy for mental acuity. It presumes that, after a certain age, an individual's mental faculties inexorably decline. In this era of advancing healthcare and longevity, this type of mandatory retirement age has questionable value. Today, it is common for individuals to remain mentally sharp in their 80s and 90s. And their experience and institutional knowledge can be extraordinarily valuable. A better approach for dealing with an individual who becomes less attentive or less effective in fulfilling their responsibilities as a trustee or other trust official is often a good process for removing them and appointing their successor.

Mandatory age caps can be useful as a part of a process by which to force the passing of certain roles to the next generation. In such instances, the age limit is part of a broader, thoughtfully constructed succession plan, rather than a stand-alone requirement. However, it still risks being a blunt-edged tool, injecting inflexibility into a structure that more often flourishes when built to be flexible and adaptable.

3.8 Designing the right process for succession (appointment and removal)

The proper design of a trust instrument should include guidance on an area that often leads to litigation: trustee succession. At a minimum, that means detailing the process for appointment and removal of trustees. But also look at the appropriateness of non-traditional considerations, such as limitations on a trustee's term of service and mandatory retirement ages. The less ambiguity, the fewer grounds for dispute.

3.9 Compensation

Trustee compensation can be a lightning rod for generating the scepticism and mistrust that often leads a beneficiary to commence litigation against a trustee. Fees and commissions can also magnify other perceived red flags in the minds of beneficiaries, once they emerge. Settlors can avoid disputes over fees in the trust agreement, with guidance from forward-thinking drafters. All too often, trust drafters use standard language providing trustees shall be entitled to 'reasonable fees'.[31] Ambiguous language like this simply kicks the can down the road, leaving the question of what is reasonable up for judicial determination – a time-consuming process that can invite

"Communication failures are a petri dish for litigation and experience has shown that few things frustrate a beneficiary more than a trustee's failure to return a call or email promptly."

dispute as to other issues with the trust or trust administration, concurrently.

Control the narrative at the outset, instead. Rather than leaving ambiguity to be determined by the court system, drafters should discuss the issue with settlors and provide guidance in the trust instrument itself.[32]

At times, settlors grapple with whether to compensate trustees at all.[33] Serving as a trustee takes time – both in tending to the affairs of trust administration and by taking time away from other endeavours.[34] Providing commissions to trustees acknowledges the effort (and sacrifice) required. It can also have a collateral effect on responsiveness. Where an uncompensated trustee is an accountant or lawyer, for example, their natural tendency may be to prioritise paying clients, at least during normal working hours. Communication failures are a petri dish for litigation and experience has shown that few things frustrate a beneficiary more than a trustee's failure to return a call or email promptly.[35] In the end, the settlor may well decide to deem certain categories of trustee (eg, family members) ineligible to receive trustee fees. But compensating fiduciaries may not only help attract good people to serve as fiduciaries but keep them more vested and attentive as well.[36]

Presuming the settlor decides to compensate the trustees, attention should be given to developing a methodology for determining what that compensation should look like. Doing so requires thoughtful engagement with the settlor and potentially a creative mindset. Some trusts and trust assets bring more daily management and administrative responsibilities than others. Even in jurisdictions where the courts have found a fee equal to a certain percentage of trust assets to be reasonable, trust assets do not always lend themselves to a ready valuation for which a fixed percentage may be appropriate.[37] Further, significant cost can be devoted to determining the valuation to which the percentage is attributed, each year. While not all trust assets are alike, settlor guidance on the issue can save significant time and cost.

In the United States, state legislatures often establish a trustee's right to receive reasonable compensation, but rarely (if ever) provide specific guidance on how that compensation should be calculated. The legislature leaves that to the marketplace and the courts tend to weigh in to provide parameters of reasonableness that are linked to fact patterns. In certain jurisdictions, trustee compensation is calculated using a percentage of assets under management. But if the sole trust asset is real estate or an art collection – as it has been in recent cases for one of the co-authors – that value can be difficult to calculate and equally difficult to pay if sufficient liquidity is lacking.

With institutional trustees and investment trust advisers, fee schedules are proposed and negotiated in advance of the engagement. The process is more contractual in nature. For individual trustees, failing to provide a methodology for calculation of the commission simply invites a dispute. In certain instances, determining the commission based on assets under management is sound – particularly where active administration and management of investments (or investment advisers) is required. In other instances, an hourly rate, time and labour, flat fee or some other methodology is a better means.[38] Providing a precise methodology in the trust instrument removes subjectivity, alleviates potential bad optics and brings more clarity for beneficiaries assessing the issue after trust administration commences.

3.10 Sharing information

A good governance structure requires the trust officials to share relevant information amongst themselves. This may seem obvious, but many trust instruments are silent on this point, and trust laws have not always clearly required trust officials to share information, although this seems to be changing. When trust officials do not share information, conditions for dysfunction are ripe. By withholding information, a trust official can impede another trust official's ability to fulfil their duties and properly administer the trust. If an investment trustee withholds information about the trust's investments, an administrative trustee may be unable to properly report to the beneficiaries. If a distribution trustee fails to tell the investment trustee about a beneficiary's financial losses, the investment trustee may fail to adjust the trust's investments to better anticipate future distributions. If a protector fails to tell the trustee about a beneficiary's change of domicile, the trustee may miss a tax reporting obligation. There are a wide range of potential scenarios where communication failures like these can detrimentally impact trust governance. Sharing information is a fundamental element of a good working relationship amongst trust officials. Lack of transparency can be a breeding ground for disputes.

3.11 Avoiding co-trustee dysfunction

Disputes are not limited to issues between beneficiaries and trustees; they can occur amongst co-trustees, as well as with or amongst other trust officials. As with family dynamics, dysfunction amongst fiduciaries can lead to mistrust and become a breeding ground for conflict. Near term, these conflicts can impede efficient and effective trust administration. If such conditions persist, however, they can undermine checks and balances within the intra-fiduciary ecosystem of the trust and ultimately lead to litigation to enforce rights, pursue surcharges or remove a trustee, among other things.

"Sharing information is a fundamental element of a good working relationship amongst trust officials. Lack of transparency can be a breeding ground for disputes."

To be at their most effective, co-trustees should each understand their respective functions within the trust and governance structure. Careful thought should be given in the drafting process to whether the trust is best served by allocating to certain trustees specific functions such as working with investment advisers, communicating with beneficiaries, disseminating required information or facilitating distributions. When trustees delegate responsibilities, best practice dictates specifying in the engagement agreement precisely what responsibilities are being delegated, what power the delegate can exercise, and how communication is to flow (eg, whether they should communicate directly with the settlor, the beneficiaries or one or more trust officers), among other things.[39] Consider whether a similar structure can be incorporated into the trust instrument that would make allocation of responsibilities as clear as it would be for delegated trustee functions.

Drafters cannot bake into the governance structure guidelines for every eventuality or co-trustee dynamic. But when there is little or no guidance, the door is open for alpha trustees to fill the void, which often means either marginalising one or more of their co-fiduciaries to the point of relative insignificance, or asserting control over specific tasks to which they may or may not be best suited. The risk is particularly acute in a multiple-trustee governance structure involving one or more non-professional trustees.

Guidance in the trust instrument alone may not be sufficient, of course. Conflict can still occur, witness a recent case involving a testamentary trust in the southern United States:

Case history: trust instrument guidance
The case involved three appointed co-trustees – two family members and the settlor's long-time accountant. The former two were both intelligent and capable individuals with advanced degrees, but no prior experience in trust administration. The latter proved to be the alpha, and he assumed an increasingly dominant role in trust administration to the exclusion of his co-fiduciaries.

Despite clear trust terms providing for equal sharing of information amongst the trustees and majority voting over critical actions (including distribution and gifting decisions), the alpha trustee embarked on a path that was dismissive of his co-fiduciaries and disregarded the express language of the trust itself. Compounding matters, he became increasingly non-responsive with his co-trustees, which heightened the sense of mistrust and concern.

The professional fiduciary's actions compelled litigation. Significantly, his course of conduct not only undermined the checks and balances embedded into the trust's governance structure, but put his co-trustees at risk of breaching their own fiduciary duties if they failed to act against him.[40]

Co-trustees each need to have a concrete understanding of their respective roles within the collective fabric of trust governance. There can be different ways of accomplishing that – including establishing committees within the trust or simply allowing the trustees to make decisions for themselves. The point here is not to suggest a one-size-fits-all approach. Instead, it is to encourage careful consideration, creativity, and active engagement with the settlor about governance during the drafting phase. Where multiple trustees are contemplated, which trustee will take the lead responsibility for communicating with beneficiaries, addressing distribution requests, or interacting with asset managers? If non-professionals are amongst the co-trustees, consider the feasibility of specific allocations of responsibility. At a minimum, articulate the settlor's intent in having one or more civilian trustees serving as fiduciaries. Similarly, if decisions are to be made by a majority vote of the trustees, consider outlining the settlor's intent and reasoning in setting such a requirement.

Some form of cost–benefit analysis is a consideration in developing a governance structure – a simple trust with a more modest asset base may not warrant multiple levels of committees and other extended infrastructure. Nevertheless, including a provision requiring regular trustee meetings can bring meaningful value, no matter how sizeable the trust. These meetings need not be monthly or involve scheduling over long weekends in wine country. Quarterly and annual trustee meetings typically suffice, at least by videoconference. Experience has shown that regularly scheduled trustee meetings facilitate effective communication and transparency amongst the trustees – two elements that can significantly aid in preventing conflict and miscommunication. Communication issues including a lack of responsiveness can detrimentally impact intra-fiduciary relationships as meaningfully as they do for beneficiaries.

4. Communicating with the beneficiaries (or not): the duty to inform and the use of quiet trusts

The duty to inform has proven to be another significant potential breeding ground for trust disputes – particularly where a beneficiary believes the trustee is not being forthright about trust holdings, performance and distributions. Generally, a trustee has a duty to keep each beneficiary reasonably informed about the trust and the material facts relating to the trust's administration. However, the trust instrument can potentially alter that obligation.

At the extreme, a settlor can establish a quiet trust. A quiet trust, or silent trust, is one in which the trustee either has a limited duty to inform – or no duty at all. The typical rationale for creating a quiet trust is that it helps to promote good character, because it insulates the beneficiaries from corruptive knowledge about their family's wealth. The underlying reasoning is that if the beneficiaries knew about their potential inheritance they would be less likely to engage in productive activities, such as pursuing education or employment. They would be more likely to evolve into 'trust fund babies'.

Query whether that rationale is logically sound. In most families, members have a general sense of the family's wealth based on the family's lifestyle. In addition, for some families, a significant amount of public information may exist about the family's wealth. Shielding family members from knowledge about a trust that holds some of the family's wealth may not be the most effective way to mitigate the potentially corrosive effects of affluence.

Reducing or eliminating the beneficiaries' right to receive information about the trust impairs their ability to ensure that the trust officials are acting in accordance with the terms of the trust. Thus, it weakens or defeats a valuable check and balance. Accordingly, if a trust instrument reduces or eliminates the duty to inform, it is essential that the trust design incorporate other methods for protecting the beneficiaries and enforcing the terms of the trust. Importantly, throttling communication from the trust officials to the beneficiaries can also lead to the beneficiaries feeling distrustful of the trust officials. That feeling can ignite fires.

In some cases, a quiet trust goes too far, tying the trust officials' hands in a manner that can be problematic. A trust instrument may contain a mandatory non-disclosure provision, which bars a trustee (or other trust official) from notifying one or more beneficiaries about the trust or its administration. Such a provision effectively precludes the trustee from seeking judicial approval of the trustee's accounts or judicial resolution of an issue. By commencing a judicial proceeding, the trustee generally must notify all interested parties, which would include the beneficiaries – whom the trustee cannot notify without breaching the terms of the trust. Such a provision may also effectively preclude the trustee from seeking non-judicial approval of the trustee's accounts or non-judicial resolution of an issue.[41] That is poor trust design.

When addressing the best approach for communicating with beneficiaries, remember that the duty to inform is firmly rooted in a public policy favouring checks and balances over power. Trustees should not have unfettered control of trust administration. Transparency is an essential means of preserving accountability and

"Transparency is an essential means of preserving accountability and keeping fiduciary actions in check."

keeping fiduciary actions in check. The primary means of keeping fiduciaries in check are the duty to inform and regular trust accountings. While the law may well allow a settlor to modify or vary[42] either of those two responsibilities, the core principle remains: transparency in trust administration must meaningfully exist to guard against bad behaviour. A trust that compromises that principle invites dispute.

Increasingly, trustees are resisting being transparent with beneficiaries – often on the basis of flawed guidance and advice of counsel.[43] Potential motivations are easy to see. The more information provided to beneficiaries, the greater the possibility of second-guessing and follow-up inquiries. Inviting protracted dialogue with beneficiaries can be a drain on a trustee's bandwidth and patience. Disparate personalities, egos, personal agendas and opinions can exist, even within the closest of families. Many trustees believe their energy should be devoted exclusively to trust administration tasks and functions, in the order they themselves have prioritised. Persistent requests from beneficiaries can be a significant distraction – especially for trustees who have other full-time jobs. But none of these practical realities alter the fundamental nature of the trustee's duty to disclose information.[44]

As a recent case demonstrates, failure of transparency also exposes trustees to the risk of creating a red flag where none exists:

Case history: transparency

Litigation against a trustee in the eastern United States was sparked by his failure to provide a copy of the trust agreement and trust administration documentation to a qualified beneficiary, as required under the state trust code. Rather than meaningfully engage with the request or explain the reason for the refusal, the trustee focused on why the beneficiary was asking for the information. "[H]aving an understanding as to why [the beneficiary] wants this information," he said, "would be helpful for me." The law did not impose a Why obligation – qualified beneficiaries were entitled to the information being sought. When the trustee dug his heels in, he found himself held personally liable for all legal fees incurred to resolve the issue. Ultimately, trust records that were produced showed no anomalies constituting a breach of trust or improper administration of trust assets. By that point, however, the damage had already been done. At each turn, the trustee's resistance bred increasing mistrust and he was ultimately removed from his role by court order.[45]

Generally, when someone is not forthcoming – whether a trustee in failing to provide a beneficiary with information about a trust, or an elected public official in failing to disclose their tax returns – the mind wanders. What has the person done that they do not wish to share? What are they hiding? Once it sets in, mistrust can have a powerful influence on future relationships and results.

5. Incorporating flexibility and adaptability into the trust

A well-designed trust incorporates flexibility and adaptability. That way, the trust can better adjust to changing laws and circumstances. There is an array of powers that a settlor should consider including in a trust instrument – or, in the case of an existing trust, that trust officials should consider adding – to facilitate this. In some cases, trust law provides the flexibility and adaptability when a trust instrument does not. In fact, one of the hallmarks of more progressive trust jurisdictions is the collection of statutory powers and non-judicial processes that enable trusts to evolve to changing circumstances.

Rashad Wareh echoes the value of building flexibility and adaptability into trust instruments:

> *I'm a big believer – whether it's a shareholder agreement, a trust or another structure – that if you want people to embrace it, they need to have some means of having 'ownership' as to how it operates .... One way you get that kind of flexibility in a trust, in terms of that ownership element ... [is] the classic power of appointment. I have some clients who come to me convinced that they don't want to provide any flexibility at all – in other words, that classic 'dead hand of the grave' is going to control it, no matter what. And usually, I can convince them that at a minimum some flexibility is needed.*[46]

Providing flexibility in the trust empowers one to address and anticipate change.[47] Consider the scenario of a settlor with three kids. One becomes a hedge fund manager; another a social worker; and the third has health issues. Having a trust with hard and fast allocation rules limits the ability to flex the trust to best serve those it is intended to serve.

> *Do you really think there shouldn't be some ability to be unequal in how things are allocated? ... [I]n terms of getting that concept of ownership ... having the ability to change [allocations], at least among family [beneficiaries], is worthwhile.*[48]

Running through potential fact-specific scenarios tailored to the settlor can prove very meaningful.

> *Once you really go through that conversation, most clients will say, [the proposed] level of flexibility is a good idea. ... I think that level of flexibility gives for those beneficiaries a feel that they actually really do have ownership in certain ways.*[49]

A well-drafted trust instrument will typically include provisions expressly granting certain powers to the trust officials that facilitate flexibility and adaptability. In a trust instrument these powers – or at least the manner in which they are exercisable – sometimes need to be balanced against settlor intent. At times, there is a tension between settlor intent and adaptability, although many of the features that enhance flexibility and adaptability can help protect settlor intent so long as they are thoughtfully designed and implemented. Significantly, the addition of provisions to enhance flexibility and adaptability – including provisions of the types discussed below – does not negate the need for meaningful checks and balances in the governance structure. Their addition should properly be considered within the broader context of the trust instrument, rather than in isolation. Safeguards and guardrails should be considered for inclusion to prevent deliberate or inadvertent actions that might undermine other protective measures in the trust.

5.1 Power to add and remove beneficiaries

The trust instrument should generally empower the trustee (or perhaps another trust official) to add and remove beneficiaries. In particular, the power to *add* beneficiaries allows the trust to evolve, expanding to benefit individuals who may have been unknown to the

"A well-designed trust incorporates flexibility and adaptability. That way, the trust can better adjust to changing laws and circumstances."

"The trust instrument should empower the trustee (or perhaps another trust official) to vary the terms of the trust. The trustee may have the power to modify the trust's administrative provisions, its substantive provisions (eg, dispositive provisions), or both."

settlor at the time of the trust's creation but become important to the settlor or the settlor's family over time. These powers are more common in trusts created outside the United States but seem to be gaining popularity in the United States as well.

The power to remove beneficiaries likewise allows the trust to evolve, by contracting to exclude individuals who do not wish to benefit from the trust. In some cases, this may be motivated by a desire to simplify the trust's administration – perhaps due to tax, privacy, or other implications of the individual changing domicile – or it may be motivated by less mundane considerations. For example, one of the settlor's children might achieve such financial success that they no longer need any of the trust's financial resources. By removing the child and the child's descendants as beneficiaries, other branches of the family may be able to enjoy those financial resources. Importantly, the removal power may enable them to achieve that result without any of the tax, legal or practical complications that a disclaimer, decanting and other strategies might present. The power to remove beneficiaries also allows the trust to evolve, by contracting to exclude individuals whom the settlor would not wish to benefit. If, for example, a beneficiary engages in activities or behaviours that are antithetical to the settlor's values, hostile to the family's harmony (eg, by injuring the family business or pursuing meritless litigation against family members), or glaringly objectionable (eg, engaging in child sex trafficking), the individual's removal as a beneficiary helps to fulfil the settlor's intent and protects the interests of the other family members who are beneficiaries.

A settlor may wish to establish safeguards or guardrails on each of these powers. For example, a settlor might grant the power to add and remove beneficiaries to the trustee but require the trustee to obtain the protector's consent to exercise that power. Some settlors limit the class of individuals whom the trust official may add as beneficiaries, but (aside from excluding a trust official who is a member of the settlor's family) this generally limits the full value that the power potentially offers.

Sometimes, tax considerations limit the use of these powers. For example, a power to add beneficiaries is inimical with a trust that is meant to be a US non-grantor trust for US tax purposes[50] or a trust that is meant to qualify for the estate tax marital deduction.[51] In these situations, taxes may unfortunately preclude the inclusion of the power in a trust instrument.

5.2 Variation or modification

The trust instrument should empower the trustee (or perhaps another trust official) to vary the terms of the trust. The trustee may have the power to modify the trust's administrative provisions, its substantive provisions (eg, dispositive provisions), or both. The broader the power to modify or vary, the more flexible the trust. Of course, the settlor may wish to establish safeguards or guardrails on this power, just as with other powers that can significantly affect the trust. The settlor should consider granting the power only to a trust official who holds the power in a fiduciary capacity. That way, the settlor helps to ensure that the power is exercised in a manner that is in the beneficiaries' best interests. Doing so would also provide a more ready means of judicial recourse to those detrimentally impacted, in the event of an abuse of the power. While granting the power to a protector (or other trust official) who holds the power in a non-fiduciary capacity may help to shield the protector from personal liability, it weakens the trust structure, potentially jeopardising the interests of those whom the trust is meant to benefit. When designing this power, the settlor might also consider whether to add a check and balance by granting the power to one trust official (eg, the trustee) but requiring another trust official (eg, the protector) to consent to any exercise of the power.

5.3 Decanting

The trust instrument should empower the trustee (or perhaps another trust official) to decant the trust. Sometimes, varying or modifying the terms of the trust is inadequate, and it is more advantageous to transfer some or all the trust property to another trust. This may be particularly so when moving the trust from one jurisdiction to another. Accordingly, decanting can be a valuable tool in trust administration. Here again, a settlor may wish to consider the inclusion of appropriate safeguards or guardrails, such as requiring the protector's consent to the trustee's exercise of the decanting power.

5.4 Changing *situs*

The trust instrument should empower the trustee (or perhaps another trust official) to change the trust's *situs*. Laws and circumstances change. With these changes, another jurisdiction may become a more attractive place in which to administer the trust. For example, it often makes sense to change the *situs* of a trust created by a non-US person after that person's death, if the *situs* is outside the United States and one or more US persons are beneficiaries. By domesticating the trust – changing its *situs* to the United States and perhaps making some other changes – the trust can avoid some onerous US tax rules that would otherwise apply.

There is a situation in which it may be advantageous to limit the trust officials' ability to change *situs*. Jurisdictions vary in the degree to which they protect settlor intent. Consequently, when protecting settlor intent is especially important (eg, because the trust instrument contains some specific provisions governing the purpose and nature of distributions), the settlor might wish to foreclose the possibility of the trust officials changing the trust's *situs* to a jurisdiction that may afford less protection for that intent. Otherwise, the trust officials' power to change *situs* can be a back door to subverting settlor intent. In such a scenario, the trust officials could change the trust's *situs* to a jurisdiction in which the laws or the courts are more likely to accede to the beneficiaries' wishes. The settlor may wish to cut off that possibility on the front end.

5.5 Changing governing law

The trust instrument should provide that, if the trustee (or perhaps another trust official) changes the trust's *situs*, then the trustee (or perhaps another trust official) may designate that the laws of the new *situs* will govern the trust's validity, construction and administration. Sometimes, the primary motivation for changing a trust's *situs* is to take advantage of more favourable laws in another jurisdiction. Often, it involves changing trustees or other trust officials, and the new trust officials may be more familiar and more comfortable with the laws of the jurisdiction in which they reside or are based. In that case, the ability to change governing law can streamline the trust's administration.

Again, the language used in granting power is important. Absent an express grant of power to designate that the laws of the trust's new *situs* will govern the trust's validity, construction and administration, the degree to which the trust officials can change the governing law may be unclear or uncertain. Some trust instruments are silent on this point. In those cases, the laws of the trust's new *situs* potentially will govern the trust's *administration*, but there may be uncertainty as to whether those laws will also govern the trust's *validity* or *construction*. Potentially worse, some trust instruments require the laws of the original *situs* to forever govern the trust's validity, construction and administration, denying the trust officials the ability to adapt to changing circumstances. This ties the trustee's hands and is not good trust design, generally.

As with changing *situs*, it may be important to limit the trust officials' ability to change the governing law if the change could subvert the settlor's intent. Like the power to change *situs*, the power to change the governing law may create a back door to undermining the settlor's intent. For example, let's consider a settlor who wishes to keep a Warhol painting in the family, and thus establishes a trust, transfers the painting into the trust and, under the terms of the trust, prohibits the trust officials from selling or otherwise disposing of the painting. Among the issues that the settlor should consider is whether to preclude the trust officials from changing the governing law if the laws of the new jurisdiction would permit the trust officials (either unilaterally or in concert with others) to vary or modify the terms of the trust to eliminate the prohibition against sale or disposition of the artwork.

5.6 Termination

The trust instrument should empower the trustee (or perhaps another trust official) to terminate the trust. At some point, the trust may outlive its usefulness. When that happens, the trustee should be able to terminate the trust and distribute the trust property among the beneficiaries. Nowadays, many trusts are designed so that they are fully discretionary, and the trustee (or another trust official) can terminate the trust by distributing all of the trust property to the beneficiaries. Of course, the trust instrument should generally modify or waive the duty of impartiality, so that the trustee is not obligated to keep assets in trust for any contingent or remainder beneficiaries.

6. Selecting appropriate liability and evidentiary standards

For which acts and omissions should a trust official be liable to a beneficiary? And what level of proof must a beneficiary meet to establish the trust official's liability? With varying degrees of certainty and specificity, the laws in each jurisdiction answer these questions, setting default liability and evidentiary standards. For example, in many US states, a trustee is liable for failing to act in good faith if the failure is proven by a preponderance of the evidence. But appropriate liability and evidentiary standards need not be left to governing bodies to determine. In some trust instruments, settlors knowingly reject the default standards under common or statutory law and set their own standards. In some cases, professional trustees demand higher thresholds, refusing to serve unless they are more insulated from liability. In other cases, the standards established under trust instruments represent form language that drafting lawyers routinely use – and do not always fully explain to settlors.

The selection of liability and evidentiary standards involves balancing the beneficiaries' interests and the trust officials' interests. As the bar for the trust officials' culpability rises, the protection of the beneficiaries' interests declines. And vice versa. When a trust official is only liable for gross negligence or wilful misconduct that is proven by clear and convincing evidence, a lot can go wrong before a beneficiary can obtain redress. A settlor may be comfortable with that, given whom they wish to have serve as trust officials and other checks and balances built into the trust instrument. On the one hand, a higher bar can reduce disputes, because beneficiaries have more limited recourse. On the other hand, it can foster disputes, because it tolerates a greater degree of bad conduct.

7. Using no-contest or forfeiture provisions to discourage disputes

Inclusion of a no-contest or forfeiture provision (also known as an *in terrorem* clause) potentially discourages litigation, but in doing so can weaken a useful counterbalance on the trust officials. Such provisions terminate a beneficiary's interest in a trust if the beneficiary commits conduct that falls within the scope of the clause, as written. Typically, that means contesting the trust or the actions of a trustee or other trust official. Consequently, for a beneficiary deciding whether to litigate or not, a no-contest provision can change the economic calculus of a dispute.

When a trust instrument does not include a no-contest provision, the downside for a beneficiary on the losing end of a trust dispute is generally equal to the legal fees incurred in its litigation.[52] In fact, in some US jurisdictions, the beneficiary's costs may be negligible because some lawyers are willing to pursue trust contests on a contingency fee basis, collecting a fee only if the lawyer succeeds in obtaining some financial benefit for the beneficiary. When a trust instrument includes a no-contest provision, the cost to a beneficiary of losing a trust dispute includes the loss of their interest in the trust. In other words, the stakes are much higher.

As such, a rational beneficiary must have a higher degree of confidence in their claim. Of course, not all beneficiaries are rational,

"Inclusion of a no-contest or forfeiture provision (also known as an in terrorem *clause) potentially discourages litigation, but in doing so can weaken a useful counterbalance on the trust officials."*

and a beneficiary who unsuccessfully challenges a trust that contains a no-contest provision, and consequently loses their interest in the trust, may turn on the advisers.[53]

A no-contest provision may neutralise an important check on the trust officials. A beneficiary generally has the right to seek judicial review of a trust official's conduct. But the existence of a no-contest provision is designed to have a chilling effect – making a beneficiary less likely to seek judicial review unless the conduct at issue is egregious. This may be especially so if, as some US jurisdictions allow, the no-contest provision applies even when the beneficiary has a reasonable basis or probable cause to initiate the contest. As a result, absent other checks and balances, trust officials may feel less constrained to avoid borderline improper conduct. Ensuring that the trust's governance structure creates effective checks and balances on trust officials thus takes on greater importance when a trust instrument contains a no-contest provision.

8. Incorporating processes for non-judicial dispute resolution

Non-judicial dispute resolution options – including arbitration and mediation – should also be vetted in trust design, as there may be significant benefits in pursuing such options, including the ability to maintain privacy and confidentiality. Contrary to common perception, arbitration is not necessarily a more cost-efficient process. However, it does bring flexibility in selecting both the tribunal and the applicable procedures, which can lead to a more expedited (and less costly) process. To reiterate a common theme, clear and concise language in constructing an arbitration provision is key. The main variables to an arbitration provision should consider a number of central criteria, including the scope and seat of the arbitration, the number and qualifications of arbitrators, the process for their selection, the arbitral institution and applicable rules and, when arbitration is made binding, the grounds required for appeal. In designing an arbitration provision, the settlor and drafting lawyer should consider the provision's enforceability under the laws governing the trust.[54] They should also consider limiting the power to change the trust's *situs* or its governing law so that a change will not adversely affect the enforceability of the arbitration provision.

Mediation is another common alternative dispute resolution (ADR) process. As with arbitration, mediation is kept out of the public eye. What transpires during mediation is confidential. Unlike arbitration, however, the mediator does not decide the merits of the case. Instead, the mediator is a neutral third party, working to facilitate agreement between the parties. Mediation has proven to be effective in achieving

"[M]ediated settlements tend to hold up over time as the parties themselves have created them."

resolution of disputes quickly – often before court proceedings commence in earnest. Further, mediated settlements tend to hold up over time as the parties themselves have created them. Significantly, a mediator can also provide an objective perspective – a reality test on each party's understanding of the strengths and weaknesses of their respective cases. In matters like trust disputes, it can be difficult for parties to be impartial or dispassionate about their claims. Mediation can also be an effective vehicle for preserving working relationships between the parties or making termination of relationships more amicable.

Dispute resolution provisions can address all or simply some issues that may arise, depending on the trust. Perhaps the trust is best served by empowering the protector to elect whether a dispute should go to ADR – mediation, arbitration or perhaps both. Creative and careful consideration and drafting of the trust document can set an overall tone consistent with the settlor's intent on the subject. In other words, ADR provisions need not be limited to a solitary captioned provision in a trust instrument. Language can be inserted in more than one place in the document, making clear that the preference is not to end up in court or in litigation and attempting to guide disgruntled parties towards not ending up in court by providing a process where they can try to resolve disputes between themselves. Including such language cannot categorically prevent litigation in every instance, but it can and does do so at times, which makes such language worth including.

9. Getting the litigator's perspective during the drafting process

Typically, trust litigators do not get the call until after a problem arises. However, experienced trust litigators can be an incredibly useful resource in trust design and creation. Simply put, a trust litigator's experience in the trenches – developing evidence, arguing over what a trust instrument does or does not state, what a trustee did or did not do, or all of the above – can be leveraged to help drafters and planners spot red flags and avoid potential disputes before they happen. Among other things, experienced trust litigators can help detect signs of diminished capacity in the settlor, challenge the qualifications of a proposed trustee, detect potential downstream issues with family dynamics, and query the appropriateness of including age-triggered distribution provisions for beneficiaries who are currently minors. Litigators who have represented both trustees and beneficiaries offer an even more unique perspective and can be used to play devil's advocate even after trust formation, when measures like decanting or trust modification are being considered.[55]

Modern trust instrument construction often reflects two acute pressure points for planners and drafters:

- externally created urgencies, often generated by anticipated tax law changes or by financial advisers with investment motives;[56] and
- the heightened commoditisation of estate planning.

The pressure to create sophisticated and effective trust documents at a competitive price point is of particular concern, as it often leads to an unhealthy reliance on form documents that are populated on a case-by-case basis, even at boutique law firms with concentrated estate practices. Estate drafting often lends itself to the use of forms, generally – tested and reliable language and structural elements that are easily understandable warrant retention. What makes the practice unhealthy is when the forms are not carefully reviewed, critically analysed, updated regularly as warranted by governing law and modern practice and, most importantly, tailored to the needs of each settlor.

Rashad Wareh explains how lawyers in his firm approach the personalisation of trust instruments so that they better articulate the settlor's intent and wishes:

> *We have two levels – our basic default language and our much more expansive language that has very detailed discussions of what 'education' means, for example. It's not just going to school – it's helping them learn and grow in certain respects. What does being 'entrepreneurial' mean? Is that a character trait you want to instill? ... I [ask clients to study the language closely] – essentially, I've given you [the client] our default language and our enhanced default language – but this is* ***not*** *where you should end. This needs to reflect* ***you****. One common problem with this is that many clients don't want to take that time. ... [But] a good number of [our clients] take on the challenge and really customize it to reflect how they approach these issues, and we help guide them in ensuring the trust language reflects their thinking ... I think having that sort of language in the trust and being very clear to beneficiaries – educating them about the meaning of that language as they grow up, making sure they understand at least what their ancestor's philosophy was. Tying that into ... that concept of ownership. I think all those things help forestall disputes.*[57]

Commoditisation critically impacts the economics for most practitioners, and often means that labour is shifted to the lowest available price point and that available time for critical assessment of a draft instrument becomes compromised. Though hard data continues to emerge, it is widely recognised that demand for trust and estate practitioners increased significantly in the United States in the aftermath of the COVID-19 pandemic-related shutdowns. Even now – as the pandemic transitions down to endemic levels – very basic errors and omissions in trust instruments drafted during that time have already begun to emerge and pose issues across the spectrum of wealth. Inconsistent and contradictory trust language, inadvertently omitted provisions on essential topics like fiduciary succession, and trust instruments providing for, but failing to name specific trust officials (eg, protectors and investment trustees) are amongst the more notable miscues of recent vintage observed by the authors. All appear to have been missed in the haste to "get something on paper" in the midst of a pandemic.

Pumping the brakes in the face of such pressure points can be challenging, particularly where cost–benefit analysis remains a constant. Trust assets are not all created equal. But if done as a matter of course, enlisting a trust litigator can prove to be a meaningful investment and important additional check and balance in the drafting process.[58] Gaining an experienced trust litigator's perspective early – having them attack draft instruments for weaknesses, inconsistencies, ambiguities, vague language or any grounds for challenge – can be a crucial investment.[59] Accepting the value-add premise for the moment, the next logical question is, when should you get a litigator involved? Look to the two bookends of the drafting process: the initial meetings with the settlor and then again once you are confident in your final draft of the trust instrument. The latter will be discussed in a later chapter. For now, let's focus on the former.

London-based trust litigator Nick Holland of McDermott, Will & Emery says:

> *I'm involved in [initial meetings with the settlor] all the time. ... I sit inside our private client team, rather than inside our litigation team – and this is a big part of the value add from doing that.*[60]

In these meetings, the partner charged with drafting the proposed trust instrument often leads the discussion by detailing provisions and measures under consideration for the settlor. Then, the impact and potential issues that can arise from moving forward with those provisions is detailed by an experienced trust litigator like Nick.

> *[Often] the settlor will push back, saying they want this control, that control ... I'll say some of these things are fine ... but* ***these*** *are the issues [in doing so], and* ***this*** *is where it can go. Cost efficiencies definitely come into play. But I think it's good value at the beginning of almost every trust we're putting together. My time sitting in your initial meeting and just cautioning you about some of the excesses that other drafters might sell you – not because they're being dishonest or not trying to do what you want. They just haven't seen what I've seen.*[61]

"Given an early seat at the table, a trust litigator is in a position to gain first-hand knowledge of the settlor's background and the purpose of the trust, as well as personal insight into family dynamics – an invaluable perspective best gained from personal experience."

Rashad Wareh agrees, citing a recent example:

> *[A]s part of the project, we deliberately hired a litigator and had them scrub the trust. It was a fascinating process, and the litigator had some very interesting comments. I wouldn't say they were big changes to the document, but there were a decent number of changes scattered throughout, tweaking words here and there, and adding a couple of concepts we then incorporated in our trusts going forward, as well. Intellectually, do I think that's a worthwhile, good exercise? Absolutely, I do. On the flip side, the disadvantage of doing so is basically two things: time and cost.*[62]

The latter is often a client concern. As for the former, Rashad postulates that adding a litigator could add a month or more to the process, which is something clients (particularly those in a rush, due to evolving health circumstances) don't necessarily want.

The practical impact of including an experienced trust litigator at the drafting stage does need to be discussed and vetted with clients in advance. But the scope of the litigator's involvement can be creatively designed. There can be significant value to the engagement, even when the litigator is not tasked with the deep dive attendant on scrubbing a proposed trust. Given an early seat at the table, a trust litigator is in a position to gain first-hand knowledge of the settlor's background and the purpose of the trust, as well as personal insight into family dynamics – an invaluable perspective best gained from personal experience. This early investment in a litigator's perspective facilitates critical, specifically tailored input into the final draft of a trust instrument to lessen the risk of disputes during trust administration.

One of the red flags that a litigator can specifically look for in those initial meetings with the settlor is signs of family dysfunction. Family dynamics are a great barometer for the threat of downstream litigation. Because dysfunction tends to fester, a drafter can implement additional measures and diligence if dysfunctional elements are identified early. This is especially so not only for high-wealth individuals but for trusts involving assets with strong emotional significance to the beneficiaries. Litigators assess credibility for a living – they assess an individual's character traits differently from those in other practice areas. This unique perspective and approach can facilitate early detection of dysfunction, which can be instrumental in avoiding later conflict.

In the drafting phase, an experienced trust litigator can be deployed to specifically look for other red flags, as well. Is there one sibling who has a dominant role in the trust? Where beneficiaries have recently reached the age of majority, are they independently represented? Is that representation meaningful? Should specialised provisions – like indemnification and no-contest provisions – specifically be addressed with them? Issues like this may seem obvious, but these are actual examples of key issues that were missed by talented practitioners and could have been caught early on.

Defined terms tend to present recurring issues, even in good times. Often, certain terms are used as defined terms but lack actual definition within the document. In other instances, terms are defined, and the definitions capitalise those terms, but the terms are not capitalised consistently (or even at all) when used in the trust instrument.

A recent matter highlighted this point for one of the co-authors:

Case history: term definition

A trust instrument was created for a settlor with unique assets, including two fully functioning aircraft from the Second World War. The extended trust agreement utilised specific defined terms that were never actually defined in the instrument. Instead, language was carried over from an earlier iteration the drafter had used on another matter, and was simply missed. The resulting ambiguities created unnecessary issues surrounding ownership and use of the assets, and delayed determination of who was responsible for payment of the costly and specialised maintenance required not only to keep the aircraft capable of safe use but also preserved from mechanical degradation.

Ambiguity in a trust agreement is a breeding ground for litigation. In this case, involving an experienced trust litigator in the diligence phase might well have caught the issue prior to execution and saved considerable resources later spent on lawyers' fees.[63]

Reliance simply on "similar language used in many prior instances" does not automatically validate that language; nor does using form language mean something was not missed. Best practice dictates carefully revisiting carry-over language every time it is used, to make certain the drafting is clear and concise, avoids misinterpretation and is effective for the specific matter to which it is being applied. Good drafting is not an easy task. It takes time, effort and thought. Investing in good drafting reduces the risk of a dispute and the time, financial cost and emotional toll that any dispute involves.

Terry Franklin, a partner in trust litigation boutique Glazier Franklin & Lodise, has this to say:

[I]f I pick up a file and find out that the drafting lawyer had consulted with a respected litigator in advance and anticipated a potential problem from a particular beneficiary and tried to draft around it – that is going to give me pause. ... [W]hen I get that email that says, "Well, I got your demand letter. I want you to know that we did run this language by [a trust litigation] expert ... who agreed that this was the best way to address this issue, or that the no contest clause in this trust was going to be useful and effective [for example]", it certainly gives me pause because I'm not necessarily going to choose to take that action or go forward with it. I'm going to have to deal with a reputable counsel who has weighed in, in advance.[64]

An experienced trust litigator can also make certain that flexibility is built into the trust structure – a critical characteristic for avoiding later disputes according to Nick Holland:

Make sure that there is some guidance that there be some flexibility somewhere in the structure – that it is not too rigid. ... [T]hat's the hardest conversation, because actually what the [settlor] wants is control. You're preaching against the grain.[65]

To illustrate the importance of flexibility, Nick cited something he sees frequently – a trust whose principal or most significant asset is the settlor's family business.

[M]ost of the disputes I deal with flow from two things: they flow from the death of the patriarch or matriarch, and they flow from the liquidity moment when they sell the family business. One of the things that I think would be most effective in avoiding these disputes is communication about what happens in the event of the sale of this asset [the family business] and building in internal flexibility to permit some degree of variation about what is going to happen with the proceeds. Part of the problem is: it's unimaginable. A lot of times, the [settlor] puts the family business into trust for the very purpose of attempting to prohibit its sale. But you do have to have a painful conversation with the [matriarch or patriarch] about the reality that that asset may one day ***have*** *to be sold. And when that happens, you may hope that this trust structure with this foundation is going to glue your family together. But certainly, here [in England] and offshore? That never works. The business will hold your family together. A good relationship amongst your family, an ability to respect one another, some flexibility in the structure – that can hold you together. But a rigid structure just designed to hold people together will fail here. And I will be in court before you're in the grave on behalf of one branch or another of your family to undo your 500-year trust. That's just the reality of it. The more rigid the*

> *structure and the less they turn their mind to what happens in the event of the liquidity moment, the more likely it is – and the* ***faster*** *– they're going to be in court.*[66]

Client urgencies (both real and perceived) are a perennial feature of an estate planner's practice. So is the risk attendant on making mistakes. Legal malpractice carriers tend to charge a premium for trust and estate practice groups for a reason. Given the asset values alone involved in working for high-net-worth individuals, the attendant exposure can be substantial. It is a recommendation that is obvious, but often overlooked: consider getting a trust litigator involved on the front end – at the planning and drafting stage, as part of the diligence team. That modest investment can provide an important and unique perspective at a critical time. As noted at the outset: preventing a fire is substantially less costly than fighting one.[67]

10. 'Failure mode and effects analysis': early detection of potential issues and warning signs

Even the best-written trust instruments can be (and are) litigated. Minimising the potential for trust disputes means including an additional layer of critical review and analysis – *after* the drafter believes the instrument is ready for execution. Once the drafter has carefully crafted the language and structure of the trust, implemented governance mechanisms appropriate to the settlor's needs, and considered all the other factors outlined above, it is essential to then assess the final draft trust document critically from two outside perspectives: the fiduciary who is going to have to administer the trust and the litigator who may be called upon to defend or challenge its terms.

Evaluating the trust document and structure for potential issues right at the outset – during the pre-execution phase and while changes are most readily made – can be instrumental in minimising the risk of disputes during trust administration. In developing an effective critical review process, consider a methodology from the field of engineering: failure mode and effects analysis.

Failure mode and effects analysis (FMEA) is a term typically associated with product design and engineering, originally used by contractors supporting the US space programme in the 1960s, then later by engineers in the design and production of a range of tangible items like automobiles and tyres. But its viability as a design tool transcends consumer products and has substantial utility as a methodology in drafting trust agreements. Simply stated, it is a proactive, step-by-step analytical method of identifying possible ways in which something might fail, assessing the impact of those potential failures, and identifying changes that need to be made. The essential idea behind the FMEA process is to put yourself in a position to act.

In the context of trust drafting, FMEA methodology is most effective when invoked during the design stage.[68] The goal is to identify possible issues and address them proactively rather than reacting to adverse events after failures have occurred or disputes have arisen:

- Does the trust agreement include all essential provisions?
- Are there omissions or contradictions in the instrument, as a whole?
- Has language been used that is capable of different or multiple meanings?
- Are the responsibilities and duties of each of the trust officers clear?
- Does the trust interact consistently with related estate documents (eg, powers of attorney) or are there potential contradictions?
- What questions or uncertainties will the current drafting generate?
- Why would or could a failure happen?
- What are the potential consequences of each failure?

The FMEA process is not a solo exercise; it is a methodology that leans heavily on interactive engagement – by its nature, it calls for different perspectives and active discourse, including differences of opinion. In the trust context, the drafter should enlist a seasoned trust litigator in the FMEA process, to weigh in on the language and structure of the final draft trust agreement and ascertain where potential issues lie.[69] Decades of trial experience have shown that estate planners, drafters and trust litigators often speak very different languages. Brainstorming with only one voice in the room (figuratively or literally) defeats the purpose. Conflicting perspectives should be embraced as an asset in critical analysis. Engage these different perspectives, recognise that even the best drafted trust instruments can be (and are) litigated, and be willing to leave any egos or pride of authorship at the door. The end goal is to effectuate the intentions of the settlor in the best way possible – and to minimise the potential for disputes and litigation during the administration.

III. Minimising trust disputes through thoughtful execution

Most of the attention in minimising trust disputes concentrates on the design phase as well as administration – and with good reason. The majority of disputes arise from actions taken (or omitted) during those two important periods. But the execution of the trust also deserves attention. Here, we briefly examine two elements of the execution process that can impact successful dispute avoidance:

- family dynamics; and
- witnessing the execution itself.

1. Family dynamics redux

Earlier, we discussed one of the red flags that can manifest as early as the initial meetings with a prospective settlor: signs of family dysfunction. But those signs may take some time to become apparent, as people are often reticent about openly airing their family's dirty laundry. A drafter or planner who remains vigilant in looking for signs of potential family strife throughout the entire evolution of the drafting process – from initial interview through to execution of the trust – stands the best chance of being able to implement additional measures and diligence to avoid disputes regarding such critical issues as capacity and intent.[70]

Particularly with high-net-worth individuals and trusts involving assets of emotional or familial significance, practitioners should maintain the same level of careful attention to family dynamics at execution as they do throughout the drafting phase. Start with the basics, then think expansively. Who attended your initial meeting with the settlor? Did someone attempt to insert themselves into your subsequent communications with the settlor? Where the settlor is older, someone may attempt to insert themselves into the drafting and execution process under the apparent guise of helping to facilitate logistics. Sometimes, the claim is innocuous and the assistance helpful; other times, that person is attempting to insert themselves into the process for some personal aim or gain. When someone attempts to insert themselves into the execution process, do you fully understand their relationship to the settlor?

Case history: the family 'friend'
In a recent matter involving one of the co-authors, a woman described by the settlor as his 'friend' attempted to insert herself into every communication he had with his counsel. In fact, she was the settlor's mistress of over 20 years. The settlor was married and had relocated his wife into an older community development overseas, in their home country.

The settlor's counsel missed obvious signs of undue influence, by failing to meaningfully inquire into the woman's background and connection to the settlor and his family.

Make certain your final meeting with the settlor prior to execution is free of any potential outside influence before the trust is executed.

2. Witnesses

During the apex of the early COVID-19 pandemic shutdowns, there was heightened discussion and concern as to how to move forward with two key elements of trust execution: notarisation and witnessing. Planners were concerned that a failure to abide by the strict language of the rules governing both could compromise the validity of a trust instrument and expose it to litigation.[71] In the United States, for example, this concern helped drive federal and state governmental enactments allowing remote online notarisation.[72] Certainly, there is potential for fraud should the rules be eliminated. But as pandemic restrictions taper and more people are engaging in person once again, it has become generally clear that there is significant interest in retaining the ability to execute documents remotely. Do the public policy concerns underlying the notarisation and witness requirements persist? If so, can they be better served in the digital era?

The subject is ripe for modern, creative thinking. While the purpose behind the notarisation requirement remains vital, the witness rule is a

"[A]s pandemic restrictions taper and more people are engaging in person once again, it has become generally clear that there is significant interest in retaining the ability to execute documents remotely."

bit of a relic. As a practical matter, witnesses are rarely a focal point in litigation or even called to offer evidence, unless an issue such as forgery emerges. Even then, witnesses are often individuals with no connection to the settlor or the trust who are enlisted (often at the last minute) to enter a room, exchange pleasantries and sign a trust instrument, acknowledging that they were present in the room when the document was signed. Even when the witness does have a personal connection to the person signing the document, the value of their having witnessed the document is often minimal. Litigation can take so long to be initiated that memories fade to the point of irrelevance to supporting a party's underlying cause or defence.[73] All of which presumes, of course, that you can locate the witness in the first place and compel them to testify.

Fuelled by the pandemic, e-signature options have magnified in utility and volume. Remote execution of documents has been made substantially easier – it can be done on one's phone using any number of apps, for example. There remain relatively few judicial decisions addressing the validity of electronic signatures, as of the writing of this book; but in the United States, the evidentiary burden attendant on authenticating evidence – for example, that an e-signature is that of the signatory – is low. Where the e-signature is backed by a digital audit trail,[74] the bar appears to be even more easily cleared in court.[75]

All of which casts upon doubt whether the witness requirement still serves the underlying public policy or whether better means exist to protect that interest.

The point here is not to encourage practitioners to summarily dispense with jurisdictional mandates.[76] But perhaps the better approach is to make the witness role more meaningful. Consider using technology to enhance the role of the witness. At times, practitioners have utilised video to capture not only the execution event, but the dialogue leading up to the moment of execution – dialogue with a settlor about key facts supporting and confirming capacity, for example. Technology can help preserve information that may not only prove useful in addressing potential disputes before litigation commences, but can be presented in court, if needed.

3. Presence of individuals other than the settlor and witnesses

When an individual other than the settlor, the drafting lawyer, or any witnesses attends the signing of the trust instrument, there may be an elevated risk that this individual is unduly influencing, or could be perceived as unduly influencing, the settlor. Neither is good. Of course, much depends on who the settlor is, and who the other individual is.

If the trustee is a bank or trust company, the presence of the institution's representative is likely fine, because there is little likelihood that the bank or trust company is unduly influencing the settlor. For that reason, their presence potentially would be advantageous. If the trustee is an individual, the individual's presence may be questionable. Is the individual a professional trustee? Is the individual the settlor's friend and business partner? Is the individual the settlor's spouse? Or is the individual a family member other than the settlor's spouse? The settlor and their advisers should carefully consider the potential for even creating the appearance of undue influence.

These same considerations apply to other trust officials and whether they or, in the case of entities acting as trust officials, their representatives should be present.

4. Self-imposed formalities

In connection with the execution of a trust instrument (or other estate planning document), some drafting lawyers include certain formalities in addition to the jurisdictional mandates. For example, the drafter may require the settlor to initial each page of the trust instrument. In such a case, the drafter typically includes a statement about initialling in the paragraph immediately preceding the settlor's signature. Although it should be self-evident, the drafter should ensure that the settlor complies with any of these self-imposed formalities. When a trust instrument states that the settlor has initialled every page – or perhaps every page other than the page bearing the settlor's signature – and the settlor has not initialled those pages, it invites questions and potentially provides a source of fuel for disputes. In those instances, the presumption is often that the omission is intentional. If it is inadvertent, the next question often becomes ... what else was missed?

5. Lifetime approval of trusts

In some jurisdictions, a settlor can commence a judicial proceeding for purposes of determining the validity of a trust that they created.[77] In effect, the settlor asks the court to declare the trust to be valid. This may be advantageous if the settlor believes that someone might contest the trust. First, it might help to discourage meritless claims concerning the trust's validity. While the settlor is living, family members and others may be less inclined to challenge the settlor's actions. As such, the request for a court declaration may proceed unopposed. Second, and more importantly, the settlor – who is the best witness about their own capacity and intent – is living and able to testify. Often, trust disputes arise after the settlor's death, and the court is left trying to discern the settlor's capacity and intent from other forms of evidence, which may be less helpful. By litigating a trust's validity during the settlor's life, the settlor may avert more protracted and expensive litigation after the settlor's death.

Naturally, there are disadvantages to commencing a judicial proceeding for purposes of determining the validity of a trust. First, it is litigation. Thus, it necessarily entails a degree of uncertainty as well as cost. Things may not turn out as planned. The hope, of course, is that it would be a better, faster and less costly result than what may happen after the settlor's death. Secondly, as a judicial proceeding it may be public. The degree to which those proceedings (and the associated filings) can remain private varies from jurisdiction to jurisdiction.

Two key considerations in preparing for the judicial proceeding are:

- Who needs to be a party to the proceeding?
- If there are persons who are not beneficiaries but who might be inclined to contest the trust in the future, how to include them as parties?

This may require some strategic thinking and may affect the design of the trust. The objective, of course, is to ensure that the court's declaration of validity binds anyone who might otherwise be inclined to contest the trust.

IV. Administration: deploying best practice and procedures

Like the design and execution phases, the administrative phase of a trust's life can create the conditions for disputes, and indeed is when many disputes arise. Accordingly, trust officials should consider what they can do to lessen – and hopefully avoid – creating those conditions in the first place. At times, that means having to take action when they are already working to resolve a dispute that has materialised. Like firefighters battling a blaze on a windy day, trust officials may have to concurrently focus on containing embers from a fire immediately in front of them, and preventing another from spreading out of control. We will examine that point – managing trust disputes – in a later chapter. Here, our focus is on how to administer a trust in a manner that saves the trust officials and beneficiaries from having any disputes in the first place. During a trust's administration, there are a number of key actions that trust officials can take to minimise the potential for disputes. They should:

- follow the terms of the trust;
- engage proactively;
- communicate with the beneficiaries;
- maintain good records; and
- critically evaluate the trust and its administration regularly.

1. Follow the terms of the trust

This may seem obvious, but experience shows that some trust officials fail even in this, the most central of tasks relating to a trust. If the terms of a trust mandate certain distributions to a particular individual, the trustee must make those distributions. If the terms of the trust allow distributions only to a specified class of beneficiaries, the trustee must not make a distribution to someone outside that class. If the terms of a trust require diversification, the trustee must diversify.[78]

When trust officials deviate from the terms of the trust, they take a perilous path. Some trust officials have ignored the terms of the trust because they were seeking to appease the beneficiaries. For some, this ended without harm (other than to the settlor's intent). For others, they found themselves having to redress their prior lapses. Although it is more typically the beneficiaries who are disadvantaged by the trust officials' misdeeds, it is sometimes the appeased beneficiaries who turn on the trust officials, asserting the trust officials should not have allowed them to benefit as they did.

To the extent that the terms of a trust are unnecessarily inflexible or restrictive – that is, certain terms are impeding the trust officials' ability to fulfil the trust's purposes – modern trust law offers an array of tools to resolve that. Ignoring the terms of the trust, however, is not one of them.

2. Engage proactively

Proactive and open engagement can prevent potential disputes from developing. The effectiveness of that engagement stems from a combination of elements, according to Sara Schroter of boutique Bermuda-based trust company, Meritus Trust:

> *It's fundamental to our business model. It's the education process, it's the family governance, it's the way we pick our clients. We want to work with families who match our values, which are centred around those things ... it's making sure that those families have got in place really strong advisers – whether it's the law firms, the investment managers, the accountants – and working as a team in one cohesive approach, especially with the family office.*[79]

Sara views empathy as perhaps the most essential value a fiduciary can bring to the client relationship:

> *We try and put ourselves in our clients' shoes and understand what the client's relationships and dynamics are, and plan and structure based on those. We look for what the values of the family are up front, so that we can help structure their trusts appropriately and everything around that, in terms of governance. So, we're very much*

led by the family, rather than by the structuring. And wherever we can, we try and jump in with the next generation [of beneficiaries] and support them.[80]

3. Communicate with the beneficiaries

Developing best practice and procedures in trust administration should be an ongoing process, and one that is subjected to regular review for improvement and refinement. One issue that can build mistrust is lack of communication by trustees to the beneficiaries. In designing a trust instrument, drafters can help settlors develop measures to facilitate communication, set expectations and perhaps make use of novel concepts like a beneficiaries committee to regularly sit down with beneficiaries; for example, to discuss investments being made and evolve from the norm of simply forwarding investment adviser quarterly reporting – some of which has lost efficacy through standardisation and self-promotion.

3.1 Ongoing due diligence

The trust officials need to know who the beneficiaries are and understand each beneficiary's circumstances. Births, deaths, marriages and divorces can change the class of beneficiaries. Similarly, when a charitable organisation is a beneficiary the organisation's merger, domestication or dissolution can affect the class of beneficiaries.

"When trust officials deviate from the terms of the trust, they take a perilous path."

"There can be significant benefits to filing trust accounts on a regularised basis that transcend short-sighted cost analysis. When left too long, trust accounts can be unnecessarily costly endeavours, as technologies change and older documents become unreadable or unavailable."

Trust officials can often perform this ongoing due diligence with an annual email or letter to the beneficiaries, although the terms of the trust may limit the trust officials' ability to communicate with them. In the email or letter, they can ask an individual beneficiary about any changes within the family. Similarly, they can ask a charitable beneficiary about any changes affecting the organisation. This simple exercise often satisfies the trust officials' duty to inquire about the beneficiaries. The trust officials should retain copies of those communications in the trust's records.

In trusts with complex governance structures, it can sometimes be unclear which trust officials have the responsibility to undertake this ongoing due diligence. Trust laws generally do not expressly address this issue, instead allowing settlors and trust officials to allocate responsibilities as they wish. Unfortunately, trust instruments do not always clearly articulate who has this responsibility.

In a trust in which the trustee does not have any discretionary distribution power, does the trustee have the responsibility to ascertain whether there have been any changes affecting the class of beneficiaries and their circumstances? Or is it the person who has the discretionary distribution power? Or both? If the trustee undertakes the due diligence (which the trustee may need to do for tax compliance and other reporting purposes), can the person who has the discretionary distribution power rely on the trustee's due diligence? Or must the person who has the discretionary distribution power independently undertake the due diligence? What about the person who has the power to invest or otherwise manage the trust property? To what extent must that person independently undertake due diligence to confirm the beneficiaries and understand their circumstances? In some cases, the trust instrument may answer these questions. In many cases, however, the trust officials must work out how they wish to tackle this. Of course, it is best to work that out at the trust's inception – and update it as appropriate – rather than after questions arise concerning the trust's administration.

3.2 Proactive trust accounting

Case history: regular trust accounting
Several years ago, the co-authors took a trust matter to trial in western Pennsylvania, on behalf of a beneficiary prosecuting various causes against three co-trustees. During a private, off the record break with counsel in chambers, the judge offered up his preference for all trustees to file an account every three years, as part of normal routine trust administration and practice. The accounting that had been filed in that case spanned decades and cost a significant amount to assemble and present. Trying to recreate a history dating back decades can be an incredibly time-consuming and expensive proposition.

As the judge noted, preparing an account every three years would likely have picked up some of the case issues early on and alleviated the significant expense attendant on trial, as well as potentially defusing the mistrust that evolved between the trustees and the beneficiary.

In the United States, the rules of procedure tend not to require accounts to be filed with such frequency (if timing is even specified). Further, trust language can specifically absolve trustees completely from the responsibility for filing accounts. There can be compelling reasons for altering trust account obligations; too often, though, language curtailing or absolving the trustees from the duty to account is inserted into a draft trust as a matter of course and passed off as standard language to the settlor (if it is specifically discussed at all). Resist the urge. There can be significant benefits to filing trust accounts on a regularised basis that transcend short-sighted cost analysis. When left too long, trust accounts can be unnecessarily costly endeavours, as technologies change and older documents become unreadable or unavailable – problems that are seen time and again in litigation. Whether at the drafting stage or during trust administration, carefully consider embracing a creative, proactive methodology instead. Preparing and filing an account every few years can be a much more productive effort than being compelled to account for administration over a 15- to 20-year period.

4. Maintain good records

An integral part of effective administration centres on modern record keeping, the parameters of which can evolve as quickly as technology. Consideration should be given to proactive record keeping on a regularised basis, even when not required by rule or law. When litigation occurs, claims can call for discovery of records dating back years and even decades. Gathering and reviewing records over such a timeframe can be labour-intensive and expensive – and can inherently lead to gaps in record keeping, which become instant fodder for trial. Towards that end, careful consideration should be given to records and information management (RIM), including records retention practices and policies, cyber-security and privacy protections. Further, good RIM practices should not just apply to the trust officials, but extend to the trust's advisers, managers and vendors to ensure that they too comply with proper guidelines.

4.1 Retention practices and policies – the 'hit by a bus' scenario

Periods of administration are essentially chapters in a larger work. In this context, maintaining proper records is essential – regarding not only administrative tasks such as transactions entered into, expenses and taxes paid and the like, but also data supporting decision making on issues including distributions, investment management and whether to provide information regarding the trust deed and trust administration to individuals claiming entitlement to such data. As a trust official you should ask yourself: If I were hit by a bus tomorrow, would trust administration continue seamlessly without me? An admittedly morbid hypothesis, but it highlights the concern. If someone had to assume your responsibilities under exigent circumstances, would your record retention practices and policies facilitate an effective transition?

4.2 Trustees and other trust officials

The trustees and other trust officials should document any changes affecting who is serving in the various roles. This may seem obvious, but gaps in the records can raise issues about whether a particular person is properly serving as a trust official and potentially, who has been delegated which specific tasks in the administration of the trust. Thus, the trust officials should document each appointment, acceptance, resignation, removal and delegation. If an individual ceases to serve by reason of incapacity or death, it is generally useful to include those details in a recitation of facts in the document appointing the deceased individual's successor. This helps to create a

"As a trust official you should ask yourself: If I were hit by a bus tomorrow, would trust administration continue seamlessly without me?"

paper trail showing the succession of persons serving in a particular role. Separately, the trust records should contain documentation establishing the individual's incapacity (eg, a statement of the physician who declared the individual incapacitated if that is the process for establishing incapacity under the terms of the trust) or a copy of an official certificate or affidavit confirming the individual's death. Consideration should also be given to the qualifications provision of the trust, and whether specific documentation or written confirmation is needed (or desired) to confirm that a person has satisfied any qualification requirements under the trust.

In some trust structures, one trust official can direct another trust official to take certain actions. For example, an investment director may have the power to direct the trustee concerning the investment and management of trust property. In these trusts, the trust officials should generally document those directions in the form of a letter, memorandum, resolution or action by consent. This may be especially important for the trust official who is following another trust official's directions, as the documentation helps to show that the directed trust official was not acting outside their scope of authority.

4.3 Distributions

A trustee or whoever has the power to make discretionary

distributions should generally document any decision concerning distributions. Banks and trust companies typically have established policies and procedures for making and documenting these types of decisions. Some individual professional trustees do too. Although many document this type of decision in a memorandum, resolution or action by consent, it is usually not the form but the content that is important. The document should generally answer three key questions:

- What prompted consideration of the distribution? For example, did the beneficiary request a distribution?
- What factors did the trustee consider when making the decision? For example, what are the relevant terms of the trust? What information did the beneficiary provide? What is the current financial condition of the trust? What effect would the distribution have on other beneficiaries?
- What was the trustee's decision?

The purpose of this is twofold. First, documenting a decision in this manner can help to ensure that the decision is well thought out and conforms to the terms of the trust. Secondly, it can help to memorialise the decision-making process, so that the trustee can better respond to any questions – perhaps years down the road – about how the trustee arrived at their decision. With trusts, the process is important.

4.4 Investments

A trust official should generally document any material decision concerning investments. As with decisions concerning discretionary distributions, banks and trust companies typically have established policies, procedures and protocols for making and documenting these investment-related decisions, as do some individual professional trustees. These decisions generally involve either:

- delegating investment powers; or
- directly exercising investment powers.

When delegating investment powers, the trust official typically has a duty to delegate prudently. The trust official therefore should document the process by which they select the delegatee and the factors that they considered when deciding to delegate investment powers. This holds true even when a trustee delegates investment powers to a co-trustee. The trust official also should document the delegation, describing within that documentation the delegation's scope and duration. The trust official periodically should review the delegatee's performance, and specifically evaluate whether the delegatee has acted within the scope of the delegation. The trust official should document both the review and the trust official's conclusions.

To the extent that the trust official directly exercises investment powers, the trust official should document any material decisions. Unless the terms of the trust require the trust official to retain specific property – such as artwork, a family villa, or an interest in a holding company or other family business – this includes the decision to retain or dispose of the property. On an annual or more frequent basis the trust official should review the investments (including any decisions concerning the retention of property). The trust official should document this review as well as the trust official's conclusions. The trust official should date the documentation so that it is clear when decisions were made, reviews conducted and documentation created. Questions about a trust's investments may arise years or decades after the relevant decision, and contemporaneously created documentation may play a vital role in preventing those questions from erupting into a dispute.

4.5 Conflict transactions

When a trust official proposes to engage in a transaction that might be a conflict transaction – that is, one in respect of which the trust official or someone related or affiliated with the trust official may personally benefit – and the trust instrument permits such transactions, the trust official should fully document the proposal and its approval. This would generally include:

- disclosure of the proposed transaction, including the information that the trust official furnished about the proposed transaction to the persons who have the power to approve it;
- the deliberative process that those persons undertook, including who participated in the discussions and any vote taken; and
- the decision that those persons made concerning the proposed transaction, including any conditions that they imposed.

Some trust instruments freely permit trust officials to engage in conflict transactions. (Query whether this is wise.) In those cases, a trust official may wish to disclose the conflict transaction – if not seek the beneficiaries' consent – because doing so may provide greater certainty that the transaction will not become a source of friction in the future.

4.6 Compensation

A trustee or other trust official's compensation can easily become a flash point for a dispute. Accordingly, documenting the process by which compensation is negotiated, established and disclosed is important.

4.7 Taxes

The trust officials should diligently document their compliance with applicable tax laws. They should also document the tax advice that they seek and receive. In addition, they should generally document how they selected their tax advisers. This is especially important when the trust faces complex tax issues.

5. Evaluate the trust and administration regularly

Each year, any number of factors can impact a trust, including changes that could potentially undermine the settlor's intent or fundamentally impact a trust official's fiduciary duties. Consequently, consideration should be given to implementing a practice that considers these issues, at least on an annual basis.[81] Proactively evaluating circumstances surrounding the ongoing administration of a trust can lead to action that heads off possible disputes.[82]

Rashad Wareh is familiar with an annual review process and sees its potential value:

> *We had an annual governance meeting [with one of my clients] recently [including] a broad 'strategic thinking' meeting that was completely focused on: is it working right? What can we make*

"Each year, any number of factors can impact a trust, including changes that could potentially undermine the settlor's intent or fundamentally impact a trust official's fiduciary duties."

better? That question is asked every year. And drawing on everyone's experience. It's not just me, but there's other key advisors that are part of this. It's really a very collaborative process. Do I think that's worth it? Absolutely. ... Conceptually, I love the idea of the annual review overview – with the right motivation.[83]

For Rashad, having the right motivation is key:

If the motivation is to make sure that this trust is functioning the best way it possibly can, to enhance the lives of the trust beneficiaries – that's a good motivation for doing it.[84]

But not if the motive is fiduciary self-preservation, "making sure the trustee won't get sued or that the trustee is not liable, if they do":

Where [the annual review process] would be problematic is when it's basically self-serving and supporting institutional fears, and essentially lets them continue to try to avoid being a real fiduciary who makes decisions.[85]

Getting the client to commit to a strategic review may be a challenge, of course. One needs to consider and balance the more obvious economic justifications – including the complexity of the settlor's estate plan and asset base, as well as their willingness to pay for such a review. There is also the matter of having the family's engagement in the process.[86]

At a minimum, the questions that follow should be explored regularly.

5.1 What has changed?

Identifying and assessing changes that may affect the trust are crucial to ensuring its proper administration. Circumstances change. Births, deaths, adoptions, marriages and divorces can affect which and how people benefit from the trust, and this in turn can affect other aspects of how the trust officials should administer the trust. A family's business may experience success or encounter financial challenges, and those changes can affect the management of business interests and other investments held in the trust. Laws also change. Legislation or case law – including changes in the tax laws – can affect how the trust officials should administer a trust.

Spotting burgeoning tension amongst the beneficiaries as part of this analysis can prove essential. Nick Holland weighs in on this point:

[T]he better private client lawyers are the ones who spot 'there's tension here' even though it may be very small. I got involved in one very large trust. Inside that trust, there was one business

> *[generating relatively moderate revenues], but it had a huge emotive value for some members of the family. A really good trustee and a really good law firm advising the family as a whole spotted the tension and realized it was not going to be easily resolved. [They] brought us in to represent that branch [of the family] and their concerns in respect to this one isolated business, in an attempt to ameliorate the problem more generally, because they quickly saw how bad this could be – that this was actually a symptom of a larger problem. There had been the liquidity moment, the father had died, they saw coming the reality that this trust might have to be partitioned. And if that happened, it could be done in a bloody fashion with lots and lots of hostile litigation or it could be done the way we ultimately did it – by way of application to the court for what we [in England] call the 'blessing of a momentous decision' which allowed the trustee to go to court and say look, the family are at risk of breaking over this. Instead of binding this family together, this structure is ripping this family apart. They could get on fine at Christmas, they could get on fine at Easter, they can have a great time together at social occasions – but what they cannot do is get together and agree on these investments with us. They are going to rip each other apart over it. We would like to partition this down into the branches of the family – the branches that agree, we'll keep them together. The branch that doesn't, we'll allow them to partition off. Had the trustee and had the private client advisors not spotted this coming or not seen how this relatively small issue could become a much larger one, it would have descended into a hugely expensive, much more divisive battle. And that would have meant that nobody is getting together for these family occasions anymore because those have been ruined by these conversations about the trust.*[87]

5.2 Would a change of *situs* be better for the trust?

Situs selection is a crucial aspect of designing and administering a trust to minimise disputes. First, there is a direct correlation between the quality of applicable trust laws and the probability of a dispute. Where applicable laws provide more certainty, there is less people can fight about. Where applicable trust laws provide a variety of tools for resolving ambiguities or other administrative problems, issues can be resolved more readily and with less risk of snowballing into a more significant dispute. Secondly, the quality of the judiciary similarly affects the probability of a trust dispute and the alacrity with which it can be resolved. In certain jurisdictions, the courts are more likely to favour beneficiaries. Lawyers know that and will try to take advantage of it when possible.

A trust instrument should include provisions allowing the trust officials to change the trust's *situs* and the laws governing the trust's validity, construction and administration, so that the trust can adapt to evolving laws and changing circumstances.

5.3 Is modification (variation) or decanting warranted?

The evaluative process may reveal that varying or modifying the terms of the trust or decanting the trust would be advantageous. Modification or decanting can be used to resolve conflict, but it can also foment it. For example, if the proposed decanting would change rights held by a beneficiary in the original trust, the decanting may be inviting conflict. Decanting can also weigh on the duty of impartiality, to which trustees are generally subject.[88]

A recent case illustrates how a decanting can exacerbate conflicts:

Case history: decanting and the duty of impartiality

In *Hodges v Johnson*,[89] the trustees attempted to use a series of decantings to avoid future disputes involving a family business, but breached their duty of impartiality when exercising the decanting power. In 2004, a successful real estate developer had created two irrevocable trusts, which he funded with interests in the family business. The trusts' key purpose was to maintain that business.

A family dispute subsequently arose. Two family members were fired from their jobs in the family business and the settlor got divorced. Through a series of decantings, the trustees eliminated four beneficiaries, including the two family members who were fired, the settlor's former spouse, and the settlor's estranged daughter. The trustees asserted that the decantings would reduce the risk of fractious litigation designed to force the liquidation of the family business. Two of the excluded beneficiaries sued the trustees, and the court ultimately voided the decantings, finding that the trustees violated their statutory duty of impartiality.[90] Notably, one trustee testified that he had not considered the beneficiaries' interests when deciding whether to decant the trusts.

Query whether, if the trustees had properly exercised their decanting power – eg, by considering the trust's purposes, considering the beneficiaries' interests and documenting their decision-making process – the decanted trust would more effectively achieve the trust's purpose and mitigate disputes involving the trust, or the family business.

5.4 Should the trust be divided into separate trusts?

Some settlors design their trusts with the vision – or, at least, hope – that a big, happy family will share the family wealth. And there certainly can be advantages to having a single trust that benefits the whole family (and possibly others). There are economies of scale in

"You can consult with a podiatrist if you're experiencing chest pains, but it probably isn't best practice. All professionals – no matter what the discipline – are not alike."

administering the trust, and there may be more investment opportunities when assets are pooled.[91] Perhaps more significantly, having a single trust potentially provides more flexibility, especially in terms of making distributions to family members who have not achieved the same degree of financial success as other members of the family. In some cases, however, the trust's purposes and the beneficiaries' interests may best be served by dividing a trust into two or more separate trusts.

Rashad Wareh offers an example, where divergent interests may create friction and the ultimate solution may be to divide the trust:

> *Say you have a trust with multiple siblings as beneficiaries – each of them with a different time horizon and different levels of needs and resources ... [T]he trustee agrees to sever the trust – to divide it between the branches and, that way, better permit the trustee to match the investment profile, needs, time horizon and so on for the various branches of the family ... [even though] this does not necessarily match with what the [settlor] had in mind.*[92]

By dividing or severing a trust, the trust officials may be able to reduce tensions among family members or branches of the family. Through the division, it may also be easier to pursue different distributive patterns for different groups of beneficiaries, implement different investment strategies, or, through the appointment of different groups of trust officials, have different groups of decision makers.

5.5 Are the right people (still) in the right roles?

People and circumstances change. Sometimes, the change is sudden. Other times, the change occurs more slowly. For example, in the case of an individual trust official, personal circumstances – such as divorce or health issues – may impair their ability to perform their duties, thus warranting a change. In some cases, a person is selected to serve as a trust official because that person has close ties to the family. Over time, however, those ties may weaken. A bank in which the family had a significant interest may be sold, and family members may cease to serve as directors. A long-time friend or business partner may drift away from the family. Of course, the change may involve the trust rather than the trust official. The complexity of the trust's activities may evolve to the point where they exceed a trust official's skills and experience to fulfil their duties.

5.6 Is your reliance on outside guidance (still) reasonable?

Trustees should periodically assess whether the guidance being provided by their outside advisers is reasonable under the circumstances.

A recent case of one of the co-authors illustrates the point:

Case history: unreasonable reliance on the advice of counsel

A US trustee based in the state of Connecticut retained his accounting firm's local commercial transactional lawyer for legal guidance as to various issues pertaining to two Florida trusts. His counsel was not licensed to practice in Florida, did not work with the Florida Trust Code, had never consulted with Florida counsel in rendering his advice to the trustee, and was providing the trustee with improper guidance as to his fiduciary responsibilities under the trust.

When an issue arose, the trustee simply deferred to his counsel, declined to obtain a second opinion on the underlying issue and found himself in breach of duty, and subject to personal surcharge and removal – all stemming from his unreasonable reliance on the advice of counsel.

You can consult with a podiatrist if you're experiencing chest pains, but it probably isn't best practice. All professionals – no matter what the discipline – are not alike. Specialisation matters, especially for disciplines involving trust litigation, fiduciary best practice and fiduciary duties. In an ecosystem characterised by the constant of

"Despite broad or express language in a trust instrument allowing complete reliance on the advice of professional advisers, rest assured: every agreement can be litigated."

billing pressures, many lawyers tend to oversell their qualifications beyond their actual areas of expertise. Many will not readily concede what they don't know, or there may be an origination credit structure within their law firm that effectively discourages deference to another colleague who is better suited to address a client's specific need. Just because a lawyer is respected in one field of law doesn't mean they are competent in specialised areas of practice like trust law and fiduciary best practice.

Despite broad or express language in a trust instrument allowing complete reliance on the advice of professional advisers, rest assured: every agreement can be litigated. Best practice dictates careful vetting of each professional during the retention process and periodically thereafter. Simply deferring to the advice of counsel without ensuring their underlying qualification to offer advice on the topic at hand exposes trustees to personal liability and the clawback of legal fees expended in the process. Verifying that counsel is admitted to the jurisdiction governing the trust instrument is low-hanging fruit.[93] If you have an issue involving a particular area of law, find counsel not only admitted in the jurisdiction but qualified to offer experience and guidance on the issue at hand.[94] Failing to properly vet counsel on a case-by-case basis can result the trustee's reliance being found unreasonable and expose the trustee to substantial personal liability. Utilise the annual systems check to assess the reasonableness of all professional guidance being provided.

5.7 Are the trust officials working together effectively?

A good working relationship among the trust officials is crucial to avoiding disputes. Are the trust officials communicating effectively? Are they each 'staying within their lanes'? If the governance structure allocates powers between trust officials, are the trust officials refraining from engaging in actions outside their respective spheres of responsibility? Conflicts can arise when trust officials fail to communicate or overstep their bounds.

Efficient trust administration can be compromised when trust officials are not on the same page about their respective functions and end results. Part of this can be addressed up front in the drafting process, by delineating some of the roles involved. But there is no substitute for experience. Given the subjective elements of each individual trust and the trust officials serving them – no matter how seasoned they may be – meaningful engagement on this subject necessarily requires experience in functioning as a unit.[95] It is also best served by including an outside perspective in the annual assessment.

Within the governing structure, trust officials either may not be able to see the wood for the trees, or may possibly feel constrained from speaking freely. Engaging an independent voice in the annual assessment process – a person outside the trust's governance structure – can be transformative. These are some of the questions to ask:

- Are all trust officials abiding by the terms of the trust?
- Does one trustee have more power and responsibility than the others?
- Do all the trust officials want to continue to serve?
- Do they have the time and capacity to continue serving?
- Have trust officials been added outside the trust agreement or since its execution?
- If so, how has the dynamic changed or impacted trust administration?
- Have the existing trust officials been properly communicating with those who were added subsequently?

An outside, disinterested voice offers a unique, high-altitude perspective that can be deployed to lead (or moderate) discussion and engagement amongst the trust officials.[96] To the extent course corrections are needed, that voice can also help facilitate documentation of the thought process behind each change, to help facilitate transition to new practices.

6. Evaluate the trust and administration when an issue arises (or maybe not)

Whether an evaluation of a trust's administration should be conducted whenever an issue arises presents a dilemma. Such evaluations can be constructive – particularly in facilitating helpful course corrections that prevent one or more issues from recurring. But consideration must be given on the front end to the timing and process involved with the evaluation, particularly where litigation is anticipated or imminent. At times, well-meaning trust officials end up implementing changes prematurely or react to the issue in a clumsy manner, inadvertently feeding the narrative of those raising the issue in the process. Obviously, not all issues are created equal. Some are minor or one-off events, while others evidence systemic issues. Trust officials should consider engaging an experienced trust litigator to provide guidance as to the path forward.

7. Utilise experienced litigators outside of litigation

Trust administration can be dynamic, irrespective of whether a dispute is active or imminent. A range of matters can arise during administration that would benefit from having input from an experienced litigator on the front end, before the fiduciary embarks on a given course of action. As Sara Schroter puts it:

New trustees' duties, high-risk asset investment, location planning, and beneficiary requests are all matters that can benefit from having a litigator involved in the discussion.[97]

Beneficiary requests can present a variety of questions for a litigator to weigh in on:

What do we think a beneficiary is entitled to? What are they going to request? What happens if they are asking to see a letter of wishes? What confidentiality can we maintain?[98] *Typically, if we see some potentially contentious beneficiary correspondence ... we'll do some planning with experienced trust litigators, to brainstorm the potential courses of action and try to de-escalate possible contention.*[99]

Distribution strategies may also call for litigator input:

For example, where we've got a big beneficiary class, what type of strategy might be put in place to ensure that we take into consideration all the relevant factors. Maybe we'll speak to them up front on that.[100]

"An outside, disinterested voice offers a unique, high-altitude perspective that can be deployed to lead (or moderate) discussion and engagement amongst the trust officials."

Trust officials are also increasingly being asked to shift investment strategies to include potentially riskier investments like non-fungible tokens (NFTs), cryptocurrency and cannabis-populated investments.[101]

> *With respect to high-risk assets – for example, cannabis or crypto – we're starting to look at more litigator involvement ... talking to the private client[102] team on the litigation side on issues like the wording of indemnity clauses.[103]*

The concern with shifting a trust's investment strategy to hold crypto is primarily twofold:

> *[O]ne is the volatility of crypto investing, generally and the other is the security – how are the coins stored? Is it using a cold or hot wallet? Who is the custodian? How much insurance coverage do they have? What are the risks? Who is taking the risk of holding the keys?[104]*

An experienced blockchain and digital asset litigator can forecast and help navigate around potential issues.

The same is true for cannabis-related investments. Fiduciaries are often challenged by the governing laws and regulation surrounding cannabis-populated investments, which can differ dramatically depending on the jurisdiction. In the United States, for example, cannabis has been legalised in some states, but not at the federal level, at least as of this writing.

> *Where we've got families in the United States who are looking at building up cannabis-populated investments in their portfolio, it presents a big challenge. So, it would help having a litigator involved to help us plan for what it might look like.[105]*

Practice groups directed towards cannabis and the hemp industry, populated with litigators, are growing at law firms around the globe.

The value of such input to trust officials isn't limited to cutting-edge modern concepts. Statutory and case law governing the interpretation and effectiveness of common trust provisions like exculpatory clauses and no-contest provisions continue to evolve. Terry Franklin comments:

> *Keeping an eye on that and having someone who's in the litigation business who is aware of the [current state of the law for a given trust provision] ... reviewing your document to make sure that you are effectively doing what the trustor wants. Because if they drafted the trust eight years ago, the law [may be] different today in terms*

of how effective the no-contest clause might be. So that's an area that I think would make a lot of sense to make sure that you're consulting with a litigator and are up to date on. It's in the statute, it's clearly defined ... but how those [statutes] have been interpreted or whether or not courts are really giving effect to the no-contest clause is something that would be useful for a planner to know as they're drafting language for a new instrument, for example, or while updating language in an existing instrument. I think the same would be true for [provisions like] exculpatory causes because case law changes and shifts ... just check in with the litigators and understand and know how well those are being used to protect the fiduciary.[106]

7.1 The devil's advocate: having a litigator review proposed changes

When contemplating proposed alterations to a trust or changes in trust administration, one should have a firm grasp on how those adjustments will be perceived by those most likely to complain about them, as well as the potential repercussions of the changes being considered. Towards that end, engaging an experienced trust litigator in the diligence process – before any changes are implemented – can prove critical, once again.

Just because you can drive a car with your feet doesn't necessarily make it a good idea.[107]

If disputes are going to arise because of proposed changes, they are going to be raised by a lawyered-up beneficiary.[108] Be proactive: hire an experienced trust litigator to play that part for you before making any changes. Engage them to critically assess each of the proposed changes as if they had been retained by a beneficiary inherently mistrustful of you or the changes you are proposing. Task them with finding issues to raise and things to dispute.

Beyond the actual changes themselves, an experienced trust litigator can help with messaging and communicating with the interested parties. Change can invite mistrust, particularly where there is a failure of communication as to the purpose of the changes. Mistrust is a contagion. Once it starts to form, it can quickly spread and make even routine actions appear nefarious. It remains one of the predominant contributors to active disputes and litigation. Once a beneficiary views the fiduciary with mistrust, the ability to establish a constructive relationship going forward may be irrevocably compromised. Trust litigators can offer distinct insight into the best means of communicating the purpose behind the proposed changes to those who will be impacted by them.

Whether modification, reformation, decanting or merger of trusts appears to be the best way forward to continue to serve the settlor's intent, or adjustments need to be made to the trust administration structure, an additional diligence process should be implemented to make certain that the changes contemplated won't lead to disputes. The devil's advocate should be an essential part of that process.

V. Reducing the risk of disputes at termination

To remain successful, athletes must remain focused from start to finish. The same is true of trust professionals. When a trust ends, the potential for disputes not only persists but may, in fact, be heightened. At least with respect to the trust that is terminating, the relationship between the trust officials and some (if not all) beneficiaries is coming to a close. In some instances, the relationship is both beginning *and* ending – a remainder beneficiary may not previously have had any relationship with the trust official, for example. During the wind-down of a trust, there is a risk that lingering tensions may boil over or new frustrations develop. Accordingly, trust officials should be attentive to both old and new relationships (and the different dynamics), and work to mitigate the possibility of ending the trust on a sour note.

For the trust officials, several questions arise when the trust ends:

- How should the trust officials approach the beneficiaries to ascertain whether they feel that they have any claims against the trust officials? If they do, how should they seek to resolve those claims?
- Along similar lines, how should the trust officials seek to ensure that, if any trust-related debts, expenses or taxes arise or are discovered after the trust property has been distributed to the beneficiaries, the trust officials do not bear personal responsibility for those amounts?

- What information should the trust officials furnish to the beneficiaries?
- Should the trust officials charge a termination fee, and if so, how much?
- When and how should the trust officials transfer property to the beneficiaries? (This is something that excites the interest of many remainder beneficiaries.)

1. Releases, judicial accountings and indemnification

Many trust officials seek certainty when a trust ends. They generally look to obtain releases for any personal liability and indemnification against any trust-related expense or liability, or they may seek judicial approval of their accounts. Banks, trust companies and other professional trust officials typically seek these protections. Family members and other non-professional trust officials are more likely to forgo releases and indemnification.

With the releases, trust officials are seeking the beneficiaries' confirmation that they do not have any claims against the trust officials (or, at least, any claims that they wish to pursue). This helps to avoid a dispute arising months or years after the trust officials distribute all of the remaining trust property to the beneficiaries. By requesting the releases, trust officials essentially force the beneficiaries into asserting any claims before a final distribution is made and while the trust officials have trust property from which to draw for purposes of seeking a resolution of those claims. Obtaining releases usually is less costly and less time-consuming than a judicial accounting.

In lieu of releases, some trust officials seek judicial approval of their accounts. This is more common with trustees than with other trust officials. While there is a long judicial tradition of trustees submitting their accounts for approval, there is limited precedence for protectors and other non-trustee trust officials doing so. Like seeking releases, seeking judicial approval of accounts generally forces beneficiaries to decide, within a compressed time frame, whether to assert any claims that they may have. As with a release, this approach aims to resolve any dispute before the expiry of any applicable statute of limitations or statute of repose. While a release requires a beneficiary's agreement, a judicial accounting does not.

With the indemnification, the trust officials seek the beneficiaries' confirmation that, as the recipients of the trust property, they bear the economic burden of any trust-related debts, expenses and taxes that may arise or be discovered after the final distribution. Trust officials will ordinarily pay or make provision for any known debts, expenses or taxes before making a final distribution. Thus, the indemnification usually focuses on unknown liabilities. Indemnification is commonly coupled with a release. If trust officials seek judicial approval of their accounts, they wind up relying on their indemnification rights under common and statutory law.

When a trust terminates, trust officials thus should think strategically about how to address any potential claims. They generally have three options. They can:

- do nothing;
- request a release and indemnification; or
- seek judicial approval of their accounts.

Although some trust officials (particularly professional trustees) have a preferred option, being thoughtful and willing to tailor their approach to the circumstances is more likely to avoid unnecessary disputes. In some cases, trust officials may start pursuing one option and subsequently pivot to another. Being flexible can allow the trust official to de-escalate a conflict.

When a trust official does nothing – that is, does not seek a release, indemnification or judicial accounting – they rely on what protections

"Many trust officials seek certainty when a trust ends. They generally look to obtain releases for any personal liability and indemnification against any trust-related expense or liability, or they may seek judicial approval of their accounts."

the law affords. With respect to claims against the trust official this is, in part, an issue of timing. A statute of limitations or a statute of repose will generally bar claims against the trust official a few months or years after the trust's termination. With patience, a trust official will typically obtain protections comparable to those of a release or judicial accounting. The trust official's main risk may be the loss of access to the financial resources that the trust would provide for defending against any claims. In some cases, the trust official can mitigate this risk by maintaining a reserve. With respect to indemnification, a trust official is generally in the same position with or without an agreement. Under common law and, in some cases, statutory law, a beneficiary generally has an obligation to refund a distribution to the extent necessary to pay trust-related debts, expenses and taxes. For the trust official, an indemnification agreement has the following advantages:

- It clearly defines the scope and duration of the trust official's right of indemnification.
- It secures the beneficiary's acknowledgement that the indemnification right exists.

When seeking releases and indemnification, trust officials should resist the urge to overreach. Some trust officials request releases that are

"Hard-nosed negotiation is generally antithetical to fiduciary responsibility."

not limited to claims related to the trust or its administration. These releases are often framed as global releases, relieving a trust official of liability for any claim arising in any capacity in which the trust official may have acted. Banks, trust companies and lawyers seem especially prone to seeking these types of releases, as demonstrated by one situation in which a co-author was involved:

Case history: choosing the right kind of release
A bank that had been serving as trustee of a family trust sought a global release from the beneficiaries, who were members of a family that had extensive relationships with the bank. The bank served as trustee of several other trusts, and it provided lending, investment and other services to the beneficiaries and other family members. The release ostensibly would have released the bank from any liability arising from those services. The beneficiaries negotiated a release that was tailored so that it would apply only to claims relating to the terminating trust.

Subsequently, the family discovered misconduct involving fees that the bank charged against various investment accounts. If the beneficiaries had not negotiated the narrower release, they would potentially have found it more difficult, if not impractical or impossible, to obtain redress for those improper fees.

When negotiating releases and indemnification, trust officials should avoid threatening the beneficiaries. Trustees generally have the following ongoing duties:

- a duty to administer the trust in good faith;
- an ongoing duty of loyalty; and
- an ongoing duty of impartiality.

Threatening to withhold a distribution unless a beneficiary signs a release, or threatening to allocate against the beneficiary's distribution all expenses associated with responding to a beneficiary's inquiries about a trustee's possible misconduct, generally violates one or more of those duties. Hard-nosed negotiation is generally antithetical to fiduciary responsibility.

Some trust instruments empower a protector to release the trustee and other trust officials. This may create additional considerations. For the protector, releasing other trust officials may involve assuming liability for their acts and omissions. The protector must consider how to address any claims against them. For the trustee or other trust official whom the protector is releasing, a fundamental question concerns the validity of the release. Does the governing law expressly allow a protector to represent and bind the beneficiaries in this manner? If so, are there exceptions? If there is doubt, a judicial accounting may be a more attractive option for trust officials seeking certainty.

2. Providing information

When winding down a trust, the trust officials should generally strive to furnish all material information about the trust's administration to the beneficiaries. The reasons are twofold. First, a trustee usually has a duty to keep the beneficiaries reasonably informed about the trust's administration. A trust official other than a trustee may also have this duty, although it may not be imposed by default by the laws governing the trust, and its scope may be narrower. This duty generally applies throughout all phases of the trust's administration – including wind-down – and continues after the trust's termination. As the final distribution approaches, the temptation sometimes is to hold back information from the beneficiaries, whether because it is easier or because the information might incite the beneficiaries. By withholding material information from the beneficiaries, however, the trustee may violate their duties. Although the courts seem to struggle with crafting appropriate remedies for breaches of the duty to inform, the trustee should be mindful that the cover-up can be worse than the misdeed. In this context, that may mean inviting harsher remedies for any other breaches that the trustee may have committed.

Secondly, the trust officials may vitiate any releases that they obtain from the beneficiaries if they fail to disclose fully all material facts to the beneficiaries. In other words, without knowledge of those facts, the beneficiaries' releases may be ineffective and the benefit of the release may be illusory. Given this, a trust official has a self-interest in furnishing information to the beneficiaries, so that they can ask questions and assess whether they might have any claims. The trust official is generally not obligated to identify specific claims that the beneficiaries may have but should provide the information in such a way that the beneficiaries can reasonably understand and evaluate it. For example, the trust official should not attempt to obfuscate by dumping raw data on the beneficiaries. Besides potentially undermining the effectiveness of any releases, this may be evidence of the trust official's failure to maintain proper records or otherwise properly administer the trust.

To the extent that the trust officials are distributing non-cash assets to the remainder beneficiaries, they should generally strive to furnish all material information about these assets to the beneficiaries. This is particularly important where the non-cash assets include items like works of art, interests in privately held businesses, or real property. As a threshold matter, the beneficiaries need to be able to assess whether they are willing to accept those distributions. A beneficiary

"When winding down a trust, the trust officials should generally strive to furnish all material information about the trust's administration to the beneficiaries."

may be unwilling to accept a distribution to the extent that they would assume a potential liability. Is a painting possibly a piece of looted art? Does a partnership create significant tax liabilities for its partners (with no obligation to make distributions to offset those taxes)? Does a building contain toxic or other hazardous materials?

Longer term, the beneficiaries need the information that enables them to protect or exploit their interests and fulfil their obligations. For example, knowing a painting's provenance enables the beneficiary to assess the painting's value and (at a minimum) enhances its marketability. Similarly, knowing the terms of a business's governing documents (including any shareholder, buy–sell or similar agreements) and its financials helps a beneficiary to determine the value of the business and the beneficiary's interest therein and to determine the degree to which the beneficiary can exercise control over the business.

Unpleasant surprises can cause disputes. Beneficiaries who find themselves in a bad situation may look to hold the trust officials accountable if they feel that the situation might have been avoided by the trust officials having done more to share relevant information. And they will judge relevancy in hindsight. Thus, trust officials who wish to reduce the risk of disputes arising after the final distribution should consider proactively sharing any potentially material information about the trust's assets with the beneficiaries.

3. Termination fees

Like trustee compensation generally, termination fees can be a lightning rod for the scepticism and mistrust that often leads a beneficiary to commence litigation against a trustee. There are two recurring issues. First, did the trustee communicate the fees to the beneficiaries? This is a communication issue, and transparency can help to head off disputes. In some cases, a trustee may have told the settlor about a termination fee but not told any of the beneficiaries. This may invite a dispute, especially if the settlor is not living after the trust terminates. A beneficiary who is surprised by a termination fee is more likely to challenge the fee. Secondly, are the fees reasonable? Beneficiaries sometimes do not fully appreciate the amount of work involved in winding down a trust, and a trustee can help themselves by educating the beneficiaries about the process and the effort. By the same token, a trustee should generally evaluate a fee in light of the amount of work performed, the complexity of the work, and current market rates, and the trustee should consider waiving a fee to the extent that it may be unreasonable.

4. Transferring assets

Beneficiaries are typically – though not universally – eager to receive their distributions as soon as possible. Beneficiaries vary in the degree to which they understand what is involved in winding down a trust. The ones who have the most limited understanding often seem to have the most unrealistic expectations regarding timing. Trust officials can help themselves by educating (or reminding) beneficiaries about the process and the timeline. They should update the beneficiaries as the process unfolds, especially if circumstances force changes to the timeline. Through this effort, they can help to set more realistic expectations. This is another situation in which good communication can help to avert disputes.

Trust officials should work to wind down the trust and distribute the assets in a reasonably expeditious manner. Steady progress generally is key. When beneficiaries see progress, they are less apt to become frustrated. Consequently, there is less likelihood of disputes. To that end, trust officials should consider making partial or interim distributions to the extent feasible. This is usually easier with trusts with significant assets. Although trust officials generally seem to prefer distributing private business interests in their entirety in a single distribution, sometimes a partial distribution can be advantageous, especially if the business makes periodic distributions to its owners. It is all about getting the property that belongs to the beneficiaries in their hands as expeditiously as reasonable.

Regrettably, some trustees seem to have adopted a business practice of purposely slow-walking the process of winding down a trust. These trustees, who tend to be large institutions offering commoditised trust services, often assign terminating trusts to a business unit that handles only account terminations. Inherent efficiencies that may be suggested by having a group concentrating solely on trust terminations are quickly undermined by the fact that wind-down teams are often understaffed and overworked. The objective is seemingly to prolong the trust's (or account's) termination, so that the trustee can collect more fees. A hallmark of this practice is dilatory responses to even basic status inquiries from the beneficiaries or their counsel. While taking a thoughtful, deliberate approach to winding down a trust is laudable, slow-walking the wind-down to collect more fees is a breach of the trustee's duties.

Trust officials are understandably wary of making a final distribution while potential liabilities remain unresolved. The judicious use of reserves can help here. The trust officials should generally be able to estimate the potential liability (including the costs of defending the trust or otherwise resolving the liability), which should enable them to determine how much they can reasonably distribute. Again, it is all about getting the property that belongs to the beneficiaries into the hands of those beneficiaries as expeditiously as reasonable. By retaining appropriate reserves, the trust officials are planning for potential liabilities while putting the rest of the assets in the beneficiaries' hands. Rather than dragging out the trust's administration, this approach often helps to tamp down potential frustrations that could lead to disputes.

"A perceptive trust official will see the darkening skies; a rational one will understand them and avoid running out into the yard with a metal pole."

VI. Managing trust disputes

Once litigation is threatened or begins, trust officials need to take a number of additional steps to effectively manage the dispute. A cardinal rule, of course, is to avoid exacerbating matters. Continue to abide by your obligations and duties, preserve and protect evidence,[109] and engage experienced trust litigation counsel.[110] For trust officials, understanding and preserving the scope of lawyer–client privilege is also an important part of managing trust disputes. In this chapter, we explore those concepts and include guidance to both fiduciaries and beneficiaries as to what each should consider doing once a dispute arises.

1. Avoid exacerbating the problem

Lawsuits involving trusts tend not to be spontaneously initiated events. Quite often, the storm clouds gather for some time before lightning strikes. A perceptive trust official will see the darkening skies; a rational one will understand them and avoid running out into the yard with a metal pole.

A case involving one of the co-authors serves as an example:

Case history: smoke without fire

A settlor established a trust, with his wife as the sole qualified beneficiary and his long-time accountant serving as trustee. During the administration of the trust, the trustee provided the settlor's wife with significant information regarding the trust, including direct access to data regarding the investment and investment performance of all the trust assets. When the beneficiary later became incapacitated, her durable power of attorney effectively placed her daughter in her shoes (as her agent) regarding all financial matters, including her rights under the trust. At that point, the principal lacked the capacity to understand, appreciate and manage her own financial affairs.

Rather than recognising the agent's clear authority under the power of attorney, the trustee immediately cut off all direct access to the trust's financial adviser platforms. When approached by the holder of the power of attorney to discuss the trust further, the trustee refused to provide her with even basic information about the trust or its assets. He compounded the problem by failing to return calls and email in a timely manner. When asked to whom he was directing his fiduciary duty to inform – if it was not the principal or the agent – the trustee declined to answer.

The trustee here created smoke where no fire actually appeared to exist. Records from the extended history of trust administration that pre-dated the qualified beneficiary's incapacity produced no evidence of impropriety in administration of the trust. But his course of conduct created mistrust, breeding concern and suspicion in the daughter's mind that the trustee must be hiding something. The trustee failed to recognise this growing mistrust, which ultimately fed a cause of action against him for breach of fiduciary duty, including breach of his duty to inform.

Mistrust can be a particularly challenging weather pattern to perceive. The best trust officials are those who are both technically proficient in the varied tasks of trust administration and adept at effectively communicating with beneficiaries. In the example above, the trustee may have been more focused on the former than the latter. How trust officials interact with beneficiaries can have a significant impact on dispute avoidance and mitigation.

Good, experienced trust litigators can play a crucial role here too, by helping to de-escalate disputes. They have the advantage of perspective – seeing first-hand the destructive emotional and financial toll that disputes often take on the participants. Whether representing a beneficiary or a trust official, an experienced trust litigator can help avoid that result. Unlike a drafting lawyer, who may have an interest in defending their work or hold too close a connection to one side over the other, a good trust litigator will focus on achieving a resolution. Disputes can easily become emotionally charged, and individuals on all sides can become wedded to beliefs and positions that may or may not be firmly rooted in logic or reason. A good trust litigator brings an appropriate degree of emotional detachment. As discussed later, when each party is represented by a good trust litigator, a resolution may be easier to achieve.

Finally, when an issue or problem arises, both sides should consider taking time out before becoming alarmist or assuming an aggressive posture. Nick Holland advocates strongly on this point, citing as an example a situation involving potential tax consequences resulting from an error or problem with the trust or its administration:

> *[The tax consequences]* ***may*** *be big – but they may be small. I've had some cases where the actual tax consequences wound up being insignificant, but everyone looked at it [initially] like, "Oh my God, it could be* ***huge****. We could be looking at 10s of millions in tax. Even though this is a sizable structure, this could create all kinds of havoc and who's going to pay this bill?" and everyone starts fighting – as opposed to just parking it.*

"Unlike a drafting lawyer, who may have an interest in defending their work or hold too close a connection to one side over the other, a good trust litigator will focus on achieving a resolution."

> *Let's figure out how big the tax loss really is. And when it's big or if it's big, then we'll fight about it. But don't start the fight now. I've had cases where ... the tax consequence turned out to be insignificant, but everyone started out fighting like mad at the thought that there* ***might*** *be a big [tax impact]. If everyone was well advised and you didn't have to have [attorneys] who desperately need the work – doing anything to generate fees – they would sit back and say, let's wait [and see how the tax picture plays out]. If there are limitations issues, we'll sign standstill agreements, we'll do whatever we need to do to park this. Let's see if we really have a problem. But I've seen a number of cases where everyone ran off and generated a problem that didn't actually exist. And so, then the fight becomes, "Oh, now I've spent all this money on lawyers." And now we have a big problem where there wasn't one.*[111]

2. Maintain open lines of communication

Once a dispute arises a fiduciary's first step, for Sara Schroter, is clear – engage with the beneficiary to understand what is driving the conflict:

> *What is the rationale or the reason or the motivation behind the confrontation? Because you shouldn't get to the dispute level, right? You should be able to proactively manage. So, the first question is – if it's a beneficiary, for example – what is really behind this frustration? Is it family relationship? Is it that they lost their job? Is it that they feel unheard? Is it that they are holding on to an old family grievance and it's motivating this action or behaviour? Even the biggest of families, when they set up the trust, they have this very clear vision of what they want the future to look like. And then as the branches mature on the family and they look back at the rationale, it's changed – they don't agree with what that initial rationale was 50 or 70 years ago. And now there's four branches of family and three generations in, and they've lost that unifying purpose. The family dynamics are changing. Sometimes it's not necessarily that they're mad at the trustee. How can the trustee help to resolve this before the buildup of frustration leads to litigation? Hopefully, you can identify what that reason is and help somewhat mitigate it before you get to litigation. Sometimes it's just listening, rather than being the summarily dismissive trustee – "No, you can't have that" – or this kind of authoritative figure. It's more like being that sympathetic figure ... "Tell me what you're feeling and how can we help and if it's within our power, we will do our best to see how we can assist." It doesn't always have to do with you [the trustee], there could be other reasons. But you have to get to that first.*[112]

Be mindful of the tone of your communications with beneficiaries after a dispute arises, as well – even when responding to the most aggressive communications. If a fiduciary is relying on counsel to correspond with beneficiaries, for example, carefully review the correspondence before it is sent. Often the best reaction to even the most argumentative communication from a discontented beneficiary is de-escalation. As Sara Schroter notes:

> *A lot of the work we do is rewriting letters that our lawyers prepare for us, because we know that an aggressively toned response doesn't help in bringing the tone back down. When we get a strongly worded letter back from our counsel, we often have to put the personality back into it.*[113]

Striking the right tone can be essential in helping to salvage a relationship before it devolves to an irremediable breakdown.[114]

Understanding and experiencing the beneficiary's tone first-hand is critical – not through email, letter or text:

> *Sometimes, I think trustees are scared to engage in dialogue on the phone or in person; they want to do everything through letters because they don't want anything they say to be misconstrued. But, as soon as you hide behind emails or letters, you can't hear that person's tone.*[115]

Equally important is the willingness to maintain open lines of communication, no matter how challenging that may be:

> *You have to be brave and courageous in some of those conversations, especially when it's younger beneficiaries and they really don't understand what your role is or they are seeing it very much from their perspective and don't have the maturity to try and see it from the prospective of other beneficiaries, other family members or even the trustee. That's the biggest lesson I've learned over the last 18 months or so is you get people who are very contentious. It's nothing that you've done, it's just their style and the history that they come with. But you still have to treat them fairly and equally – as fairly and equally as you treat the other beneficiary who is so lovely to you and you know their kids' birthdays and they call you up for a chat. But you have to treat everyone equally. Fairly. That's quite a hard lesson, especially when you're new to a relationship or you haven't built up that trust level with those individuals. How do you maintain that?*[116]

3. Taking a thoughtful position

A trustee should carefully evaluate any potential or actual dispute involving the trust, and should determine what position to take with respect to the matter. When doing so, the trustee should view the matter through the lens of their duties to the beneficiaries. In some cases, a trustee should take a neutral position with respect to the outcome of the dispute. For example, a trustee would ordinarily be neutral as to whether one individual is another individual's descendant and thus qualifies as a beneficiary of the trust. Similarly, a trustee would ordinarily be neutral concerning the interpretation of an ambiguous provision that, depending on how it is read, grants the power to remove a trustee either to the settlor's spouse or the settlor's children.

In other cases, a trustee's duties demand that the trustee pick a side. A case involving one of the co-authors illustrates the point.

Case history: taking a side
A married individual established an irrevocable trust, appointing a bank as the trustee. Under the terms of the trust, the trustee had to distribute the trust's income to the settlor's spouse during her life. Upon her death, the trust ended, and the trustee had to distribute the remainder of the trust property among several beneficiaries. The settlor's spouse was considerably younger than the settlor and in good health, so the settlor expected that she would outlive him. Alas, the settlor's spouse died only a few years later, dashing those expectations.

When the trustee subsequently stopped distributing the income and began the process of winding up the trust, the grieving settlor objected. Despite the clear language of the trust instrument, he insisted that the trustee continue distributing the trust's income – albeit to him rather than his deceased spouse. Saying that it was "neutral" in the matter, the trustee suspended its efforts to wind up the trust and told the settlor and the beneficiaries that they would need to resolve what should happen with the trust. The settlor sued the trustee and the beneficiaries. After a trial, the judge ordered the trustee to distribute the trust property to the beneficiaries. The judge also admonished the trustee for breaching its duty to act in the beneficiaries' interests

Once a dispute arises, Terry Franklin looks to two critical tasks, each of which provides a foundation for a thoughtful approach going forward. First, he examines the current practices and procedures of the trust's administration:

> *[Review] the procedures and practices of the fiduciary quickly, to see whether [the trustees] ... had a process in place for making sure that administration was proceeding appropriately. Because the evidentiary issue is always going to be, "What was the process in*

place?" or "Was there a procedure in place and was it followed?" As opposed to simply looking at what the result was at the end of the day. When a beneficiary says, "Your investment strategy was inappropriate" – it's the strategy that matters and not the results. So, I think going back and reviewing – when the storm clouds begin to rise from the beneficiary – how has the trustee behaved? How much notice has been given? Has the trustee been providing accountings on a regular basis? Were there any questions or potential red flags that were not disclosed adequately? Those would be the kinds of questions I'd want to know the answers to early on, so I can anticipate how we're going to get ourselves out of this situation sooner rather than later. How did we get here? Perhaps it's an unreasonable beneficiary who's been consistently asking for and demanding information well beyond what was presented. [The trustees] have been giving them information and yet we know that this is a litigious person who has got someone – it's often a family member – who is encouraging them to keep nudging and asking those questions. Can we figure out a way to neutralize those concerns early on before it [leads to active litigation]? And maybe that means having a meeting or scheduling a meeting where we try to air whatever the potential issues are before it rises to the level of litigation, before it gets to that point.[117]

The second critical task for Terry is an extension of the concept discussed above: looking at whether forgetting, neglecting or perhaps stalling in the execution of one's fiduciary duties has exacerbated or compounded the initial problem. Once a dispute arises, Terry recommends reminding the fiduciary what their obligations are, that their fiduciary obligations continue to exist, and that their purpose is really to look out for the interests of the beneficiaries. As he notes:

In a lot of the family situations that we see come up, the family member fiduciary sees themselves in the role of being paternalistic or making decisions on behalf of the beneficiaries that don't respect the beneficiary's own points of view. [Family member] fiduciaries often forget the need to really be scrupulous about communicating with beneficiaries in a way that is impartial ... because they have some [personal or familial] connection to them. Of course, the trustors knew when they were creating the instrument that this relationship might end up impaired ... they know when they choose the surviving spouse as the trustee, for example, that there may be a potential conflict with beneficiaries. That's there from the very beginning. That's part of the reason why it's important for us to remind the fiduciaries of the fact that their role is defined by the trust instrument and by the law and that, if they haven't been complying with that, they need to be.

> *Professional financial institution trustees – we often see those entities being in a sort of paternalistic relationship with the beneficiaries, where they don't take into consideration the fact that those are individuals with individual feelings and some level of concern needs to be applied for that. You just can't [take an authoritative approach:] "I'm the trustee and I'm going to keep moving these levers just as I always have", even when the beneficiaries are raising issues about whether they're behaving properly.*[118]

Nick Holland cites two early considerations as key to developing a thoughtful position:

> *A big part of it is making sure you [as fiduciary] understand who's hostile to you. It's rarely going to be the entirety of the beneficial class. It is more likely it is some, but not all these people. And if you see [the dispute] coming, try and make sure [the beneficiaries] have separate, good representation you can recommend to them – people you know are going to give good advice that they need, but people who are also going to be sensible and understand the area. Don't let them run off and hire somebody who is otherwise chasing ambulances. It is very difficult even for wealthy people to figure out who a good lawyer is. Don't pick some stooge who is going to do what you [or the fiduciary] say. Pick a good lawyer who knows the area, but who can sort this out. Give [the beneficiaries] several names, tell them you're going to get good advice from this person, go talk to them.*[119]

Nick's second point may seem counterintuitive to some, but has proven true for the co-authors, as well:

> *I'm not trying to influence the outcome [in doing so]. I don't want that lawyer to come back and say there's no problem. I want that lawyer to be a good lawyer, who gives good advice to those people and that's it. Typically, you'd probably give them three names – you'd say, look here's three people. They are good in this area. Check out everything you can about them. But here's a lead on three people who really know what they're doing. Talk to them.*[120]

When a beneficiary is working with a lawyer who has limited or no experience with trusts and trust litigation – a personal injury lawyer is a classic example – the beneficiary may not get good advice and thus may have unrealistic expectations about the range of potential outcomes. Working with counsel who lacks specialisation in the trust space can prolong the litigation and increase the attendant emotional and financial costs. Further, when a trustee is working with a lawyer who has limited or no experience with trusts and trust litigation, the results can be worse. Trust litigation is unlike commercial litigation. A trustee (or other trust official) who engages in aggressive litigation tactics may violate their fiduciary duties in doing so. For example, a trustee's duty to inform does not end when litigation begins. A trustee who uses the discovery process as a shield against providing information to the beneficiaries may breach the duty to inform.

For Rashad Wareh, a thoughtful position for fiduciaries includes thinking creatively about the end result:

> *If there is a dispute, you need to ... be open to a resolution that will actually include your resignation, as long as you get released. Too often, when it actually does end up in litigation, I think it's because there's a real feeling that the trustee just wants to stay connected [to the trust] for the income stream. If they really wanted to resolve the dispute and if the relationship has broken down to the point where this is even an issue, they should at least be considering resignation as long as an appropriate successor is being named that would respect the [settlor's] intent. But [instead], they cling to [the role].*[121]

Trust litigation is a specialty practice area. When one side lacks the guidance of someone with expertise in the space, inefficiencies often emerge, constructive engagement tends to stall, and disputes languish unnecessarily. The ability to minimise the impact of a trust dispute can be significantly influenced by having experienced trust counsel involved on all sides.

4. Preserving lawyer–client privilege

With sound legal advice, a trust official is better equipped to fulfil their duties and the trust's purposes. Sound legal advice can help to avoid improper conduct, and craft an appropriate solution if it has already taken place. Sound advice requires an open dialogue between a trust official and their lawyer. As one jurist wrote:

> *[T]he purpose of the attorney–client privilege is to encourage full disclosure of information between an attorney and his client by guaranteeing the inviolability of their confidential communications.*[122]

In addition to the customary admonishment to avoid disclosing privileged communications to third parties (and thereby waiving the privilege), trust officials must consider the effect of the venue (or potential venue) for trust litigation and the implications of the appointment of a temporary or successor trust official.

For trust officials, the jurisdiction in which trust litigation occurs can affect whether lawyer–client privilege applies. In the United States, some courts have adopted the fiduciary exception. Under that exception, privilege does not apply to communications between a trust official and the trust official's lawyers.[123] Some states have statutorily rejected the fiduciary exception.[124] If a trust's *situs* is in a jurisdiction that applies the fiduciary exception or a trust official either resides or has a principal office in a jurisdiction that applies the fiduciary exception, then lawyer–client privilege may not apply.

Trust officials must also be mindful of how the appointment of a temporary or successor trustee may affect the lawyer–client privilege. In trust litigation, a beneficiary may request the appointment of a temporary trust official who would serve during the pendency of the litigation. A temporary trust official, however, may have the power to waive lawyer–client privilege with respect to communications between the predecessor trust official and the predecessor trust official's lawyers.[125] Similarly, a successor trust official may also have that power.

5. Litigation management

When trust disputes arise, attention (and frustration) often focuses on the attendant cost. Lawyers, accountants and other professionals can

> *"Mediation and arbitration are the two most utilised extrajudicial dispute resolution processes, and both tend to lead to a resolution faster than litigation."*

generate a significant cost in fees when a dispute arises, which spikes even further when litigation is fully underway. Trust disputes are not cheap and almost always diminish trust assets to varying degrees.

Even in jurisdictions where they are allowed to tap into trust assets to fund expenses for legal counsel, trust officials need to remain cognisant of the expenses being incurred by the trust and actively manage the professionals they retain.[126] Any personal benefit that accrues to trust officials under such circumstances is not outweighed by the obligation to preserve trust assets.

No matter how personal a dispute can seem to the individual, a trust official's duties with respect to the trust do not go on hiatus. Engagement letters with counsel (and other retained professionals) should specifically detail the scope of the relationship and work being performed, and the hourly rates and expense provisions; and invoices should be sufficiently detailed (in time and task) and carefully reviewed before payment. Though the focus is often on hourly rates, high litigation costs are more frequently a by-product of hours expended and the number of timekeepers billing to the file. Ask for regularly updated litigation budgets[127] and have the engagement letter:

- identify which timekeepers will be working on a given matter at the outset; and
- require counsel to obtain your pre-approval before adding more timekeepers later.

Engage with counsel and take an active role in strategy and decision making regarding issues such as the identification of fact witnesses and retention of experts.

Avoiding protracted litigation is often the end goal in effective litigation management. Prompt resolution of the underlying issues can limit the expense and personal toll often attendant on trust disputes. Towards that end, ADR options may be available and provide a more cost-effective path forward. Mediation and arbitration are the two most utilised extrajudicial dispute resolution processes, and both tend to lead to a resolution faster than litigation. The primary difference between the two is the process. Mediation is a non-binding process typically conducted by a single mediator who facilitates discussion amongst the parties to reach a meeting of the minds. Mediators are not fact finders; they do not 'judge' the merits of a case. Arbitration is typically a binding process that replaces a full trial in court with one or more arbitrators who are chosen by the parties to preside as judges, hear and make rulings on the evidence, and decide a case on its merits.

Communication between counsel and trust officials on issues including strategy and dispute resolution remains as critical for trust officials and their counsel and other professionals as it does in the other relationships discussed throughout this book.

6. Advice for beneficiaries when a dispute arises

Maintain open communication. Take a thoughtful position. That guidance can apply to beneficiaries as well as trust officials once a dispute arises. But practitioners interviewed for this book offered specific advice, as well.

This is from Sara Schroter:

> *The first thing is to gather information and to understand what information you are entitled to as a beneficiary. Because some beneficiaries seem to be scared of trustees – "Oh, I can't possibly go and ask for that." No, you* ***can*** *ask for a copy of the trust deed. You* ***can*** *ask for records of accounts in whatever form that looks like. You* ***should*** *be introduced to the trustee – if you are a beneficiary of a trust, you should be having a relationship with the trustee because they should understand your personal circumstances. So, collect the information you're entitled to, get it reviewed with a trust lawyer – not your best mate, but somebody who actually understands what they're talking about, which involves spending money. If you're serious about this, you need to get the right information, get the right advice, understand your rights, and build a relationship with the trustee. A trustee doesn't want to be deliberately unhelpful to a beneficiary, by and large. Be open with your communication. And talk to your family. If the issue is something to do with your dad, and there's a relationship there, talk to your dad directly. Start with that; you don't jump to litigation. As trustees we often play the role of mediator, but where possible we encourage and facilitate direct dialogue between family members as a starting point along with the other relevant stakeholders. Sometimes litigation is inevitable, but there may be other ways of coming to a satisfactory resolution for all of the parties.*[128]

Terry Franklin has this advice:

> *Really carefully document [your] experience with the fiduciary, so that I have a record by which to understand what information has and hasn't been disclosed to [you,] the beneficiary – focusing on things like when [you] first became aware of the concerns, so that we don't find ourselves prohibited from raising issues, either because of a statute of limitations issue or because it's been disclosed in an accounting or otherwise. [And] try to maintain a good relationship with the fiduciary in the hope that the fiduciary will be more willing to share the information that we're going to*

need to develop to pursue [the] case. Rather than shutting the trustee or fiduciary down, so that they go into defensive mode immediately and leave it to formal discovery, which is going to be more challenging and more expensive for the beneficiary. I've certainly told beneficiaries on more than one occasion before they hired me – talk to the trustee. Ask them if they're willing to share more information with you, so that you try to maintain their positive relationship to the extent you can and gather as much information so that we can objectively assess the potential for the litigation. How likely are we to get a good result at the end depends on how much information we have at the beginning.[129]

Nick Holland's advice:

Two things. Is there an amicable solution that can be obtained right now, before everyone has spent a fortune on lawyers? Because very quickly, we're going to spend a lot of money and some easy resolutions that may have been available will have been lost. Is there a solution right now or one that with a little bit of digging could be obtained? Is there an easy win here? [Second is] making sure they have very realistic expectations: this is going to cost an awful lot of money [to litigate]. It is going to have a hugely emotive component, because you are going to be having to litigate with family members. If you are really up for this, then that's fine. But just know what you're getting into and make sure there are no quick wins. Those are the two most important things I can communicate with them [the beneficiaries]. If we're going to be having a real fight, then we need to talk about how we secure the information we need because that's going to be our next problem. And making sure you constrain them. There have been some cases over here, in that kind of setting, people ran off and did things that wound up causing huge damage. For example, raiding a family member's computer and unlawfully taking information which created enormous havoc. ... Let us worry about how we obtain information. Don't you go off and do something that will come to haunt all of us. And don't destroy anything. What documents and information do we need, what information and documents have we got – and do not have a bonfire.[130]

And this from Rashad Wareh:

On the beneficiary side, their weakness is they think they are right and they want acknowledgment of that. They want to win that acknowledgement. That's just jousting for pure justice. They need to look for positive change that they can live with – aim for what's important to them, accomplish it and move on, and not get bogged down in emotions. [Inherent in this is leaning on the advice of good, experienced trust litigators.] I think litigators are really good about not getting bogged down in the emotional side of things. The planners almost have too close a relationship. Half of my practice is emotional and it's hard to disengage with that sometimes.[131]

VII. Conclusion

The emotional, financial and opportunity costs of trust disputes can be staggering. Preventing fires – and thus the imposition of those costs – is a multi-faceted effort. For the family office working with the family to establish and administer their trusts – especially trusts intended to hold the family's wealth for multiple generations – minimising the risk of trust disputes starts with thoughtful trust design and formation. It continues with establishing and implementing processes for administering the trusts, including a continuous process for evaluating and adapting the trust structures. Thoughtful design, formation and administration are crucial measures for preventing fires. Open communication between the family office, trust officials and beneficiaries can also often play an important preventative role. Despite even the best efforts, a fire may still ignite. At that point, it is vital that the trust officials avoid adding fuel to the fire. At the first sign of a potential dispute, they should engage an experienced trust litigation lawyer. And even though they may feel under attack, they must faithfully fulfil their duties and preserve evidence.

By doing so, they will be better able to avoid a conflagration.

Notes

1 Interview with Terry Franklin, 16 February 2022. Terry Franklin is an experienced trust litigator, a Los Angeles-based partner with trust litigation boutique law firm, Sacks Glazier Franklin & Lodise.
2 *Ibid.*
3 Though the level of family wealth deemed 'high net worth' or 'ultra-high net worth' vacillates, traditional family offices have historically been the province of families with total net worth north of $100 million (around £80 million).
4 The problem can be particularly acute depending on the nationality of the family involved, where culture differences and concepts of privacy can be complicating factors. Trustees can find themselves repeatedly explaining the concept of fiduciary responsibility to an audience with a steep learning curve. If not done properly, there is a greater potential for contention, because it can incubate significant misunderstanding.
5 Interview with Nick Holland, 24 February 2022. Nick Holland is a London-based trust litigator with global law firm McDermott, Will & Emery.
6 *Ibid.*
7 UK Criminal Finances Act 2017, c 22 (Eng). Available at: www.legislation.gov.uk/ukpga/2017/22/contents.
8 In response to increasing compliance burdens, some trustees have increased their fees. In turn, some families have changed trustees, appointing lower-cost providers. Query whether, in at least some cases, this is a short-term saving with costly long-term implications. Is the lower fee indicative of a more efficient operation? Or perhaps of a trustee that is subject to less extensive or stringent compliance obligations? Or of less robust compliance efforts or less skilled and attentive trust services? As we note throughout this book, one of the challenges facing families and trust officials is the commoditisation of trusts. That challenge is not the exclusive province of the instruments themselves. The commoditisation of trust services can present its own challenges. As we discuss later in this chapter, some trust service providers are wrong for the job. In addition, to the extent that some trust service providers are enabling or facilitating the flow of illicit funds, this understandably fuels interest in legislative and regulatory efforts to expand compliance measures even further. When enacted or adopted, those measures in turn increase the burdens – and costs – on innocent beneficiaries and legitimate trust structures.
9 Trust officials may enjoy protections against liability for certain compliance obligations. In the United States, for example, a financial institution is generally immune from civil liability for filing a suspicious activity report (SAR) with the US Treasury Department's Financial Crimes Enforcement Network (FinCEN). These protections, however, are limited. Trust officials must generally fulfil their compliance obligations without any special protection against liability (whether for failing to properly administer the trust, breaching privacy or something else).
10 Sometimes, a lawyer writes an overly long trust instrument as a way of showcasing their knowledge. The trust instrument is a testament to the drafting lawyer. Sometimes, a lawyer writes an overly long trust instrument out of a fear of missing something – for example, adding special needs provisions even though no one in the settlor's family has special needs. The lawyer's insecurities – perhaps coupled with a lack of time for thoughtful reflection or a lack of substantive knowledge, or both – leads them to write an engorged trust instrument. This ironically may foster more problems than it avoids.
11 Interview with Rashad Wareh, 3 March 2022. Rashad Wareh is a partner with Kozusko Harris Duncan in New York.
12 *Ibid.*
13 Communication issues and lack of transparency can breed mistrust amongst co-trustees, as well, as discussed below.
14 Sometimes, the settlor intentionally disenfranchises their children (and other beneficiaries), granting control exclusively to the trust officials. This often (but not universally) reflects the settlor's patriarchal views toward family. Other times, the settlor unintentionally disenfranchises the beneficiaries. The settlor may not fully appreciate the trust's governance structure and, in particular, what – if any – procedures exist for the removal and appointment of trust officials. Sadly, this seems to occur more frequently when a trustee or other trust official is the drafting lawyer.
15 Interview with Rashad Wareh, 3 March 2022.
16 The focus of this conclusion has been on what is known in the United States and elsewhere as the 'baby boomer' generation – those born between approximately 1946 and 1964 – who are retiring in increasing numbers, with greater wealth and potentially more diverse familial circumstances than the generation before them.
17 Alzheimer's disease is a neurodegenerative condition that typically starts slowly and progressively worsens. See: World Health Organization, "Dementia", September 2021, available at: www.who.int/news-room/fact-sheets/detail/dementia. The early symptoms of neurodegenerative diseases such as dementia or Alzheimer's are frequently mistaken for normal ageing. See A Burns and S Iliffe, "Alzheimer's Disease", *British Medical Journal* 338:b158, February 2009.
18 Some may have difficulty separating out the emotion attendant on a past event (such as marital infidelity or divorce) or cling to long-held convictions as to the invincibility of a parent despite strong evidence suggesting their conviction is now misplaced.
19 For discussion of drafting to protect settlor intent, see Todd D Mayo, "Protecting settlor intent", *The International Family Offices Journal*, December 2018, pp30–37.
20 Warren E Buffett, preface to *A Plain English Handbook: How to Create Clear SEC Disclosure Documents,* US Securities and Exchange Commission, 1998, p1.

21 Though the plain English concept is well developed, convoluted provisions continue to find their way into legal documents, including trust instruments. In a recent matter involving one of the co-authors of this book, opposing counsel proposed language in a trust-related document that began with a sentence comprising over 200 words. Sentences of that length invite ambiguity, among other things.
22 See, eg, Bryan A Garner, "Learn Them and Ax Them", *ABA Journal*, April 2014, pp26–27; Bryan A Garner, "Shall We Abandon Shall", *ABA Journal*, August 2012, pp26–28; *Bayerische Landesbank v Aladdin Capital Management LLC*, 692 F 3d 42 (2d Cir 2012) (construing the word 'herein' in a contract); *Weichert Co of Maryland, Inc v Faust*, 419 Md 306 (2011) (construing the word 'hereunder' in a contract); *Trustees of First Union Real Estate Equity & Mortgage Investments v Mandell*, 987 F 2d 1286 (7th Cir 1993) (construing the word 'thereof' in a lease agreement); and *Raine v Drasin*, 621 SW 2d 895, 905 (Ky 1981) (Lukowsky, J dissenting) (criticising the use of 'and/or'). Disputes involving the construction of contracts can be instructive in drafting trust instruments.
23 Interview with Rashad Wareh, 3 March 2022.
24 *Ibid.*
25 For a discussion of trust governance models, see Todd D Mayo, "Trust Governance Models", *The International Family Offices Journal*, June 2017, pp28–38.
26 In this example, drafting lawyers can potentially avoid the issue by querying at the outset whether it is optimal to exclude the younger beneficiaries, rather than allowing their parents or other representatives to act on their behalf.
27 Recent matters have affirmed the significant role a protector can play – and a lack of understanding as to how they function within the trust administration structure (by people who should know better). The role of protector should be explained fully to the settlor at the outset and, as with other key elements of trust construction, the protector selected purposefully. Best practice for litigation avoidance is for the protector role to be served by an individual completely independent of each trustee and not under the control of the drafter/planner. Doing otherwise is often perceived as a red flag and a potential source of conflict.
28 For experienced estate planner Rashad Wareh, two guidelines readily come to mind when selecting the right governance structure. "In terms of avoiding disputes, I'm a big believer in not forcing people to work together where that is likely going to generate friction, if the client's willing to let you prepare for a division. I will also usually not have a sibling be a fiduciary for another sibling's trust. I find that's a very frequent source of unhappiness." Interview with Rashad Wareh, 3 March 2022.
29 For an in-depth discussion of private trust companies, see Todd D Mayo (consulting ed), *Private Trust Companies: A Handbook for Advisers*, Globe Law and Business, 2020.
30 The laws governing the trust's validity, construction and administration determine the degree to which a trust official can act in a non-fiduciary capacity. Jurisdictions like the Bahamas and New Hampshire statutorily recognise non-fiduciary trust advisers and protectors and have judicial traditions that provide a high degree of confidence that a trust provision governed by those statutes would be respected. In other jurisdictions, the lack of well-developed law poses a risk that a trust adviser or protector may have a non-waivable fiduciary status.
31 A surprising number of trusts are silent altogether as to whether compensation is permitted.
32 Compensation is not exclusive to trustees. Settlors should consider whether it is appropriate to compensate protectors for their work on behalf of the trust, as well.
33 If the settlor decides not to compensate the trustees, then consider stating so expressly in the trust instrument. Otherwise, the risk is run of creating a void in the language that could lead to litigation.
34 Commissions are not necessarily exclusive to trustees. Compensating protectors remains an important question, too – and one that is often overlooked. Earlier, we detailed the critical role a protector plays in a well-established trust governance structure. While investment advisers and other support elements are compensated via outside engagements and fee agreements, protectors are often overlooked despite undertaking roles that can require significant time and specialised attention.
35 This is particularly so when modern email platforms allow the sender to receive an automatic return receipt showing when the trustee opened their email.
36 Whether a trustee or other trust official is being compensated – and factors like the level of compensation and whether it was reasonable – may also impact a court's willingness to impose personal surcharge or other monetary damage awards against a trustee or other trust official for breach of fiduciary duty or to enforce an exculpatory clause. Terry Franklin is a name partner with the boutique trust litigation law firm, Sacks, Glazier, Franklin & Lodise in Los Angeles, who has concentrated his practice in the area since the early 1990s. As Terry notes (in interview, 16 February 2022):

> *If you're compensating [a trustee], you increase the likelihood that you'll get their attention – but it also increases the level of responsibility and accountability and should ensure that [the trustee] will give [whatever matter or concern is being raised] the attention and focus that is required. Whereas, if you have a fiduciary that's a family member, who's not compensated, they certainly have the ability to say, "I wasn't even taking a fee for this. This was something I was doing out of the goodness of my heart." When a judge looks at that, the judge can say, well, they weren't being compensated, so we're going to give them a break. But the flip side of that is: you were uncompensated and therefore it's giving you free reign to misbehave or to not be studiously*

focused on your responsibilities as a fiduciary. ... [I]t almost seems like the judge should come down harder on that person, to discourage them from either taking on the responsibility in the first place or to make sure that they are compensated, so that you increase the likelihood that they're being attentive to their responsibility and understanding the importance of this fiduciary role that they are playing.

37 Where the sole asset of a trust is a deceased artist's collection of works, for example.

38 Also, to trustees: when entitled to compensation, arrive at a schedule for when the fees will be paid and make certain the payment occurs. All too often, trustees take a cavalier approach to collecting fees to which they are entitled. Many then request payment of accrued commissions all at once, in an account or in reaction to litigation – as though deferring collection of the commissions provided for in the trust is a defence to improper behaviour or will make them appear more sympathetic to a fact finder. Neither is the case.

39 Indemnification is another frequent topic, as is confirmation of the delegate's privacy and security policies, whether the delegate has vetted standards (and insurance) to protect against cyber-security issues and maintain privacy of confidential trust information, and, if the delegate is regulated, whether other applicable standards are set and remain met for the duration of the engagement.

40 Intra-fiduciary disputes can raise a range of separate issues, as well. Is it appropriate to pay fees and costs associated with prosecuting such an action from trust assets? What about costs of defending against such an action? Is it appropriate for both sides of a dispute to tap trust assets to fund their respective litigation costs, even just in the near term (ie, prior to settlement or adjudication)? What is the impact of applicable indemnification provisions? Can intra-fiduciary disputes reach a point where a trustee risks violating fiduciary duties directed to protecting and preserving trust assets from diminution?

41 In some cases, the trust instrument designates a person to represent one or more beneficiaries, and the trustee provides any notices and reports to that person. This representative may be a protector or, in some jurisdictions, a designated representative. By using a representative, the settlor potentially addresses the concern about whether providing the beneficiaries with information about the trust and its administration would have a detrimental effect on the beneficiaries or the trust's administration, while requiring the trustee to be accountable to someone. Of course, the efficacy of this approach depends on its design and execution. Some key questions: What is the representative's incentive to act in a manner that protects the beneficiaries' interests? Is the representative a fiduciary who owes a fiduciary duty to the beneficiaries? If the representative is a fiduciary, does this approach merely serve to shift liability for a trustee's breach of trust from the trustee to the representative? If the representative is not a fiduciary, does this approach effectively absolve everyone of liability?

42 In the United States, practitioners refer to 'modification' of a trust, whereas outside the United States, the term to describe the same action is 'variation'. The terms are used interchangeably in this book.

43 This topic is discussed in greater detail below, in the discussion of annual evaluations.

44 The issue of to whom the duty is owed is a recurring source of litigation. In one recent case, standing was raised as a defence when an agent under durable power of attorney sought certain information from the trustee as to a trust of which the principal was the sole beneficiary. The principal had been receiving regular information about the trust from the trustee, predominantly by email. When the principal ceased to have capacity, her agent assumed control over her email account. When the trustee learned that the agent was then receiving the information, he cut off email access and ceased providing any information to the beneficiary directly. The ensuing legal action exposed the trustee further when it was revealed that his decision to cut off the principal's email access meant he was no longer providing information about the trust to anyone, in breach of his duty to inform.

45 The trustee's refusal to provide information included dismissing the beneficiary's suggestion that the parties seek a third-party legal opinion on the issue, to avoid court intervention.

46 Interview with Rashad Wareh, 3 March 2022.

47 *Ibid*. Rashad also had this to say:

For attorneys, I think the advice is: build in a good decanting provision. ... Not that you can [be unfettered]. Not that you can use the power to add anybody on the planet that you want. But just a good solid decanting provision. One of the reasons we don't see disputes escalating to litigation that often is because when there has been stress between trustees and beneficiaries ... as long as the trustee is willing to bend at all – between decanting and getting a release so the trustee knows they're not liable – we've usually been able to solve every issue that's come up.

48 Interview with Rashad Wareh, 3 March 2022.

49 *Ibid*.

50 IRC § 674.

51 IRC §§ 2056(b)(5) and (b)(7).

52 The beneficiary's own legal fees, in jurisdictions applying the American rule, or both sides' legal fees, in jurisdictions applying the English rule.

53 See, eg, *Tamposi v Denby*, 136 F Supp 3d 77 (D Mass 2015).

54 In the United States, states like Arizona, Florida, New Hampshire and South Dakota have enacted statutes making arbitration provisions in trust instruments enforceable: Ariz Rev Stat § 14-10205; Fla Stat Ann § 731.401; NH RSA 564-B:1-111A; and S D Codified Laws § 55-1-54. In some states, the courts have addressed the enforceability of such provisions, with mixed results. For example, in Texas, the

state's highest court held that they are enforceable: *Rachal v Reitz*, 403 SW 3d 840. In contrast, in California and Georgia, courts have held that they are not: *Diaz v Bukey*, 125 Cal Rptr 3d 610 (2011) and *Boyle v Anderson*, No 210392 (McCullough) (Va 14 April 2022).
55 This topic is discussed more fully below.
56 The increasing popularity of trust instruments – fuelled by both the ongoing battle amongst trust jurisdictions to make themselves the most desirable trust *situs* and a heightened interest in confidentiality, particularly for international wealth – does not mean that those pushing for them understand what they are or what they do. In the race to manage assets that may be considerable, many financial advisers exert significant pressure on drafters to rush to create boilerplate trust instruments to fuel investment management objectives ... without understanding how trusts work or the duties of trust administration.
57 Interview with Rashad Wareh, 3 March 2022.
58 If your practice compels a level of nimbleness that creates a reliance on forms, or cost–benefit analysis otherwise precludes the addition of a trust litigator in every instance, enlisting an experienced trust litigator even just to review your process of using your own form language on a regularised basis is best practice. Litigators are called upon to either attack or defend trust language and administration. What better way to strengthen the steel of your practice than to seek out those whose role is to undermine it?
59 Interviewed on 16 February 2022, Terry Franklin said:

> *I've always thought that it really makes a whole lot of sense for [fiduciaries] to consult with litigators in advance so they can anticipate the kinds of arguments that are going to be made by that disgruntled beneficiary and try to get the language right. It always seems like a good idea to me ... if you have questions about how something might be interpreted, you should consult with a [litigator]. ... We do find ourselves in situations where we come in after the fact and say, "If you had considered changing this language or making this adjustment, we would have been in a better position." [A]s a personal matter, I think it makes a lot of sense to consult with the litigator, if you can get that point of view in advance.*

60 Interview with Nick Holland, 24 February 2022.
61 *Ibid.*
62 Interview with Rashad Wareh, 3 March 2022.
63 Drafters should create and supply to trust officials searchable PDFs of original executed trust documents, at least as a complement to hard copy material being provided to each. The completeness of an electronic document search is only as good as the inputs. So, before finalising and circulating documents, use variations of the term you are searching to account for misspellings. When done correctly, having the ability to quickly search a document electronically can help trustees rapidly locate where a given term is used and defined (or not) within a trust agreement. Searchable PDFs are also incredibly helpful tools for prospective trustees, as they review trust documents and assess whether to accept a fiduciary role for a given trust.
64 Interview with Terry Franklin, 16 February 2022.
65 *Ibid.*
66 *Ibid.*
67 Interviewed on 24 February 2022, Nick Holland said:

> *When I first came to the United Kingdom [over a decade ago], I never understood why I was getting pulled into meetings [with prospective settlors] all the time – and this was why. I was getting pulled in to tell disasters, so that people say, "Oh, I really do need good quality advice. Otherwise, it's this guy." And of course, it is absolutely true that [litigation is] tons more expensive than getting your planning right.*

68 Implementation during the design stage is important, but a solid critical review process can bring considerable value during trust administration, as well. When used as part of the annual evaluation process (discussed in a later chapter), the FMEA analytical approach can help not only to mitigate the risk of trust disputes during administration but to facilitate continuous improvement in trust drafting more broadly.
69 In an earlier chapter, we explored the benefits attendant on engagement of a seasoned trust litigator in the planning and drafting process. The most critical moment of engagement, however, is when the drafter believes the final draft of the instrument is ready for execution by the settlor.
70 This same care and best practice should be adhered to in any efforts to amend or vary a trust.
71 There may be exceptions, of course. As a situation in which one of the co-authors was recently involved illustrates, some planners elevate expediency over formality. In that situation, the drafting lawyer acted as both a witness and the notary public taking the witnesses' acknowledgements.
72 See, eg, Margo HK Tank, David Whitaker, Elizabeth SM Caires and Andrew Grant, "Coronavirus: Federal and state governments work quickly to enable remote online notarization to meet global crisis", DLA Piper Alert, 15 August 2021. Available at: www.dlapiper.com/en/us/insights/publications/2020/03/coronavirus-federal-and-state-governments-work-quickly-to-enable-remote-online-notarization/.
73 Recently, one of the co-author's clients was subpoenaed as a third-party witness, in part to testify about documents she witnessed a parent sign two decades earlier. She recalled nothing about the event (including even witnessing the execution) and had no information either regarding the content. Her testimony on the subject was limited to confirming that the signature appeared to resemble that of her now-deceased parent.
74 Audit trails are digital records collected and maintained by an e-signature service provider that

identify such information as the names, email addresses and unique signing identifiers of signatories, as well as time-stamped information to trace when (and even where) a signatory receives, views and executes a document, using IP addresses and other identifying data.

75 See, eg, *Schrock v Nomac Drilling, LLC*, 2016 WL 1181484, at *3 (WD Pa 28 March 2016); *IO Moonwalkers, Inc v Banc of America*, 814 SE 2d 583 (NC Ct App 2018); *Simple Global, Inc v Banasik*, CA No 2018-0809-PAF (Del Ch 24 June 2021).

76 Likewise, the point is not to encourage practitioners to become complacent when clients dispense with jurisdictional mandates. During the pandemic, many individuals executed trust instruments and other estate planning documents without the drafting lawyer's supervision. This seems to have led to more instances in which individuals failed to follow the requisite formalities. Although the courts might be forgiving, given the circumstances, the drafting lawyers might help their clients and their families avoid headaches and disputes by proactively reviewing the documents that their clients signed without their supervision. Through this process, they might identify documents that ought to be re-executed or for which other remedial actions might be advisable.

77 See, eg, NH RSA 564-B:4-406(d): "During his or her life, a settlor may commence a judicial proceeding to determine the validity of a trust that he or she created, subject only to the trust's subsequent amendment or revocation if the trust is revocable."

78 In many trusts, a trustee is subject to a duty to diversify. Under the governing law or the terms of the trust, this duty usually does not require diversification in all situations. Instead, it usually requires diversification unless the trustee determines that, because of special circumstances, the trust's purposes would be better served without diversification.

79 Interview with Sara Schroter, managing director, corporate and general counsel of Bermuda-based private trust company Meritus Trust, 11 February 2022.

80 *Ibid*. This support includes Meritus University, a company-driven education platform to educate beneficiaries on subjects such as Trust 101 and Investment 101.

81 In an earlier chapter, we reviewed the use of the FMEA analytical process in trust creation, leveraging different perspectives to analyse a draft trust instrument critically and proactively for defects or issues. FMEA's utility is not limited to the design stage, however. The methodology can also be used during an annual or regular strategic review to help analyse how trust administration has been progressing, where changes can be made, and whether the trust and trust officers continue to serve the settlor's purpose and the terms of the trust itself.

82 Few would contend that case law interpreting trusts transforms at a blistering pace. It tends to evolve more gradually. But current triggers for trust litigation – those actions, emotions and circumstances that motivate beneficiaries to pick up pitchforks and torches and storm the castle – refresh regularly and are often entirely avoidable. Trust litigators see them in real time and can identify potential triggering events proactively. The frequency of common, repeatable issues underscores the need for and value of a regular review, in good economic times and bad. Involving a seasoned trust litigator in the annual assessment process can help further mitigate the risk of one of those triggers being pulled.

83 Interview with Rashad Wareh, 3 March 2022.

84 *Ibid*.

85 *Ibid*.

86 "I've seen clients who have trouble [with even routine administrative asks] each year and they spurn your help in doing *that*. I'm not saying that all clients are like that, but that is a challenge." Interview with Rashad Wareh, 3 March 2022.

87 Interview with Nick Holland, 24 February 2022.

88 Under this duty, a trustee must treat each of the beneficiaries fairly, considering their interests in making decisions that may affect the beneficiaries differently. For example, a trustee must consider the other beneficiaries' interests when making a distribution to one beneficiary or when making an investment decision that might favour one beneficiary or a group of beneficiaries over the others. Fair does not mean equal. However, it does mean that the trustee considers all of the beneficiaries' interests.

89 *Hodges v Johnson*, 170 NH 470 (2017).

90 On this point, the court's opinion seems to ignore the express terms of the trust. The trust instruments seemingly waived the trustee's duty of impartiality. See *Hodges v Johnson, ibid* (the trustee had the power to decant into a trust "for the benefit of any one or more, but not necessarily all, of the group consisting of [the settlor's spouse] and [the settlor's] descendants, or any trust established by [the settlor] under another trust instrument for the benefit of any one or more, but not necessarily all, of the members of such group").

91 Maintaining a single trust to pool investments is not always necessary. Multiple trusts can potentially use a partnership or other entity to pool investments and, through such a structure, gain access to investment opportunities that they could not access separately.

92 Interview with Rashad Wareh, 3 March 2022.

93 Lack of admission to the jurisdiction is not necessarily a deal breaker. Is the lawyer aligned with counsel in that jurisdiction? Does the lawyer have colleagues or co-counsel available to them who are admitted there? The recommendation here is to ask pointed questions and actively vet counsel, rather than presuming an lawyer has the expertise needed to give effective guidance on the issue at hand.

94 Obtaining a written legal opinion can bolster your claim to reasonable reliance on the advice of counsel. But do not merely rest on its receipt. Carefully review the opinion piece and ask follow-up questions, where needed. If uncertainty persists, get a second opinion.

95 This is equally so after trustee turnover. Successor trustees inherently alter the dynamic – for both good and bad.
96 Having a disinterested voice can be critical in constructive assessment of current trust administration processes, as well. If the trust document calls for delegated trustee powers to be documented and formalised, for example, is that being done consistently? Are the documents supporting those designations being appropriately retained? Are record retention, confidentiality and cyber-security policies being adhered to?
97 Interview with Sara Schroter, 11 February 2022.
98 Here Sara Schroter referenced *Schmidt v Rosewood Trust Ltd* (Isle of Man) [2003] UKPC 26 (27 March 2003), which addressed a beneficiary's right to information regarding a discretionary trust. The decision effectively held that trustees faced with a request for information regarding a trust must weigh various relevant factors before deciding whether to accede to the request (and what information to provide). The decision was subsequently adopted into English law in *Breakspear v Ackland* [2008] EWHC 220 (Ch).
99 Interview with Sara Schroter, 11 February 2022.
100 *Ibid.*
101 Investment strategies may be impacted by a shift to other vehicles, as well. For example, interest has been steadily increasing in environmental, social and corporate governance (ESG) investment opportunities. Where a subset of beneficiaries would like to be more sustainably invested, and the trust is transitioning particularly to the next generation, the current duties of a trustee relating to shareholder capital growth may impact the ability to invest in those ESG businesses that draw diminished returns. Planning around that may benefit from litigator involvement.
102 Law firms sometimes designate this practice group 'private wealth services', 'private client advisers' or similar.
103 Interview with Sara Schroter, 11 February 2022.
104 *Ibid.*
105 *Ibid.*
106 Interview with Terry Franklin, 16 February 2022.
107 Paraphrasing Chris Rock from *Chris Rock: Bigger & Blacker*, 1999 TV Special, CR Enterprises, 3 Arts Entertainment, Production Partners, Inc, Home Box Office.
108 Often, these disputes are a complete surprise to the fiduciary. In numerous instances, proposed modifications that appeared to be rational proved to be so disruptive with the beneficiaries that they were not worth the effort in implementing them.
109 Once on reasonable notice of imminent or potential litigation, an affirmative legal obligation may be imposed on trust officials to preserve and protect records. Remember that communications on any platform – including video and digital platforms – are potentially discoverable forms of communication, at least in the United States. At time of writing, that would include text messages, voicemail and app communication platforms such as WhatsApp, Telegram, Messenger, WeChat, Viber and KakoaTalk. It also includes platforms that may not immediately come to mind, including video conferencing apps such as Zoom, Microsoft Teams and Skype (including communications posted in chat rooms), as well any other platform where visual and textual communication can occur, such as SnapChat, Facebook and Instagram. The conservative approach is to presume discoverability of all communications and social media posts, no matter what the platform. If it's out there, a motivated litigator may well find it.
110 In interview on 11 February 2022, Sara Schroter offered this advice for fiduciaries:

> *Get really good legal advisers early on. Choose a law firm that you'd like to work with and build a relationship with them such that you've got the firm on speed-dial, and you can call them as soon as (or before) an issue kicks off and have pragmatic discussions with them: we have this issue – what do you think we should do? How should we handle the next correspondence? At the end of the day, we are always looking to do what is in the best interests of the beneficiaries and so you want to work with advisors who understand and value that.*

Terry Franklin (in interview on 16 February 2022) agrees:

> *Absolutely. ... We have had some situations like that where we've been able to come in early, have a conversation with the fiduciary and address the issue with the beneficiary before it becomes a bigger issue. When you can do that and you have a good relationship with the fiduciary, that makes a whole lot of sense.*

111 Interview with Nick Holland, 24 February 2022.
112 Interview with Sara Schroter, 11 February 2022.
113 *Ibid.*
114 The decision to assume an aggressive tone at the outset is often client driven. Rashad Wareh (in interview on 3 March 2022) adds that an experienced trust litigator can serve an essential role in de-escalating one's own client:

> *[Good] litigators actually know what really happens in a dispute. Non-litigators may have some experience [with litigation] if they've touched upon it from time to time, but don't really know. So, I think [having a litigator involved] just goes straight to de-escalation. And I've seen it happen with one of my clients, where I relied on a fiduciary litigator ... in part, to be able to basically tell the client yes, we could proceed. Here's what that is going to look like. Here's what is going to happen to you in that process. Even if you win, just how brutal it's going to be to get there. And the likely cost. If it had been only up to the client? [The client] was ready to litigate. ... What the litigator did extremely well was walking [the client] through that thought process. That is a form of de-*

escalation – de-escalation through fear or through the realization that just because you think something is 'just', you don't necessarily pursue litigation.
115 Interview with Sara Schroter, 11 February 2022.
116 *Ibid.*
117 Interview with Terry Franklin, 16 February 2022.
118 *Ibid.*
119 Interview with Nick Holland, 24 February 2022.
120 *Ibid.*
121 Interview with Rashad Wareh, 3 March 2022.
122 *Riddle Spring Realty Co v State*, 107 NH 271, 274 (1966).
123 See, eg, *Riggs National Bank of Washington v Zimmer*, 355 A 2d 709 (Del Ch 1976); *Wells Fargo Bank v Superior Court*, 22 Cal 4th 201, 212–213 (2000); and *Hammerman v Northern Trust Company*, 329 P 3d 1055 (Ariz Ct App 2014).
124 See, eg, Fla Stat Ann § 90.5021(2); NH RSA 564-B:2-205; and SC Code Ann § 62-1-110.
125 In New Hampshire, a temporary or successor trustee does not have the power to waive lawyer–client privilege with respect to communications between the predecessor trustee and the predecessor trustee's lawyer, unless the predecessor trustee consents. See NH RSA 564-B:2-205(c) and (d).
126 While some trusts and jurisdictions may provide for trust officials' expenses to be advanced by (or indemnified from) the trust, courts can enter surcharge or other monetary awards that compel trustees to reimburse the trust.
127 Such budgets can be an inexact science, given a certain level of uncertainty and unpredictability inherent in litigation generally. Nevertheless, they can be an effective means of keeping litigation costs out in the open and in check when appropriately managed.
128 Interview with Sara Schroter, 11 February 2022.
129 Interview with Terry Franklin, 16 February 2022.
130 Interview with Nick Holland, 24 February 2022.
131 Interview with Rashad Wareh, 3 March 2022.

About the authors

Todd D Mayo
Executive director and senior wealth strategist, UBS
todd.mayo@ubs.com

Todd D Mayo is an executive director at UBS, where he is a senior wealth strategist in the firm's Advanced Planning Group. In that role, he works with ultra-high-net-worth families, helping them to design and implement wealth strategies that reflect their goals and values. He helps them create multi-generational structures for managing their wealth, fulfilling their philanthropic visions and optimising tax consequences.

Before joining UBS, Todd was general counsel of Perspecta Trust. He was previously a partner in Cleveland, Waters and Bass and before that served as president of Cambridge Trust Company of New Hampshire. Prior to that he practised trust and tax law.

In addition to his role at UBS, Todd is an author. He is the consulting editor of *Private Trust Companies: A Handbook for Advisers* (Globe Law and Business, 2020) and a contributing author of *Advising the Wealthy Client: A Handbook for Working with the Ultra Wealthy* (Globe Law and Business, 2020) and *Beneficial Ownership Registers: The STEP Handbook for Advisers* (Globe Law and Business, 2021). He has also written numerous articles. These include articles on trust governance structures and protecting settlor intent in *The International Family Offices Journal*. Other articles have appeared in *Estate Planning*, the *STEP Journal*, *Trusts & Estates* and *Trusts & Trustees*.

When he was a practising lawyer and trust company executive, Todd helped write many of New Hampshire's laws governing trusts and trust companies. Notably, he was a principal author of the New Hampshire Family Trust Company Act (which governs private trust companies) and the New Hampshire Foundation Act (which was the first act in the United States recognising civil law-style foundations).

Todd earned a BA in economics and history from Georgetown University, a JD from the University of California, Hastings College of the Law, and an LLM (taxation) from the University of Florida.

Kevin W Rethore
Managing partner, Caffrey Hill, PLLC
kevin.rethore@caffhill.com

Kevin W Rethore is an experienced trial lawyer representing high-net-worth individuals and families, leading businesses and fiduciary clients based in the United States, Europe, Asia and the Middle East. After 25 years of practice, including almost two decades with two of the world's largest multi-national law firms, Kevin became managing partner of Caffrey Hill, PLLC – a boutique law firm that represents an intentionally limited client base in complex litigation. In addition to an active trial practice, Kevin serves certain clients in an outside general counsel role, advising on crisis management and litigation strategy, litigation preparedness and risk mitigation.

Kevin's career put him in court early, successfully bringing his first case to verdict less than one year into practice. He has since chaired more than 85 trials and arbitrations and argued before state and federal appellate courts across the United States on critical issues, including multiple appeals directed to the scope of personal jurisdiction in an evolving global economic landscape. Amongst other experience, he was a co-author of the Petition for Writ of Certiorari that led to the seminal 2011 US Supreme Court decision, *Goodyear Dunlop Tires Operations, SA v Brown.*

Immediately prior to joining Caffrey Hill, Kevin was a shareholder at Greenberg Traurig (GT), where he conceptualised, developed and launched the firm's fiduciary litigation practice group alongside firm leadership. He joined GT in 2018 after more than 15 years with leading global law firm DLA Piper LLP, where he represented clients in high-profile trust litigation, auditors in high-exposure professional liability and fraud litigation, and Fortune 100 companies in catastrophic product liability actions.

Kevin has served as an impanelled arbitrator and third-party neutral mediator on matters including a range of trust disputes. He currently serves as a trust officer on multiple trusts, as well as on corporate and non-profit boards.

Kevin earned a BA in English from Boston College and a JD from the Dickinson School of Law of Penn State University, where he served as an editor of the *Dickinson Law Review.*

About Globe Law and Business

Globe Law and Business was established in 2005. From the very beginning, we set out to create law books which are sufficiently high level to be of real use to the experienced professional, yet still accessible and easy to navigate. Most of our authors are drawn from Magic Circle and other top commercial firms, both in the UK and internationally.

Our titles are carefully produced, with the utmost attention paid to editorial, design and production processes. We hope this results in high-quality publications that are easy to read and a pleasure to own. Our titles are also available as ebooks, which are compatible with most desktop, laptop and tablet devices. In 2018 we expanded our portfolio to include journals and Special Reports, available both digitally and in hard copy format, and produced to the same high standards as our books.

In the spring of 2021, we were very pleased to announce the start of a new chapter for Globe Law and Business following the acquisition of law books under the imprint Ark Publishing. We are very much looking forward to working with our Ark authors, many of whom are well known to us, to further developing the law firm management list, and to welcoming our new Ark customers.

We'd very much like to hear from you with your thoughts and ideas for improving what we offer. Please do feel free to email me at sian@globelawandbusiness.com with your views.

Sian O'Neill
Managing director
Globe Law and Business
www.globelawandbusiness.com